The Theory of Consumer Demand:

A Critical Appraisal

PRENTICE-HALL INTERNATIONAL SERIES IN MANAGEMENT

BAUMOL *Economic Theory and Operations Analysis*

BROWN *Smoothing, Forecasting and Prediction of Discrete Time Series*

CHURCHMAN *Prediction and Optimal Decision: Philosophical Issues of a Science of Values*

CLARKSON *The Theory of Consumer Demand: A Critical Appraisal*

CYERT AND MARCH *A Behavioral Theory of the Firm*

GREENLAW, HERRON, AND RAWDON *Business Simulation in Industrial and University Education*

HADLEY AND WHITIN *Analysis of Inventory Systems*

HOLT, MUTH, MODIGLIANI, AND SIMON *Planning, Production, Inventories, and Work Force*

MASSE *Optimal Investment Decisions: Rules for Action and Criteria for Choice*

MILLER AND STARR *Executive Decisions and Operations Research*

PFIFFNER AND SHERWOOD *Administrative Organization*

PRENTICE-HALL INTERNATIONAL, INC., UNITED KINGDOM AND EIRE

PRENTICE-HALL OF CANADA, LTD., CANADA

C. BERTELSMANN VERLAG, GERMANY AND AUSTRIA

DE BUSSY, HOLLAND AND FLEMISH-SPEAKING PART OF BELGIUM

DUNOD, FRANCE AND FRENCH-SPEAKING PART OF BELGIUM

HERRERO HERMANOS, SUCS., SPAIN AND SPANISH-SPEAKING COUNTRIES OF LATIN AMERICA

MARUZEN, FAR EAST

The Theory of Consumer Demand:

A Critical Appraisal

Geoffrey P. E. Clarkson

School of Industrial Management
Massachusetts Institute of Technology

Prentice-Hall, Inc.,   Englewood Cliffs, N. J.

PRENTICE-HALL INTERNATIONAL, INC., *London*
PRENTICE-HALL OF AUSTRALIA, PTY., LTD., *Sydney*
PRENTICE-HALL OF CANADA, LTD., *Toronto*
PRENTICE-HALL FRANCE, S.A.R.L., *Paris*
PRENTICE-HALL OF JAPAN, INC., *Tokyo*
PRENTICE-HALL DE MEXICO, S.A., *Mexico City*

Library of Congress Catalog Card Number 63-10541

Printed in the United States of America
C

Preface

This essay is not a treatise on classical theories of consumer behavior. Instead it is an inquiry into the possible existence of an empirically testable theory of consumer demand. The inquiry begins with an examination of currently received theory and ends with the outline of a proposed theory of consumer decision-making behavior. My object, then, is to discover whether it is possible to construct a micro-economic theory of consumer demand that can be submitted to a series of empirical tests. Since theories that are not empirically testable cannot be employed to generate empirically significant predictions, the motivation for this study is clear. It is provided by a desire to explain and predict consumer behavior.

It is a pleasure to acknowledge my indebtedness to Professors C. G. Hempel and H. A. Simon. While the extent of my debt is partially apparent from my references to their published work, I particularly wish to express my thanks to Professor Hempel for his many helpful comments and criticisms.

Since parts of this book are based on a previously published article, I would like to thank the editors of the *Industrial Management Review* for their permission to borrow freely from this earlier publication.

Finally, I should like to thank the Social Science Research Council for making it possible for me, under a Post-Doctoral Fellowship, to spend a year in the Department of Philosophy at Princeton University studying the problems posed in this essay.

G.P.E.C.

to **MAX** and **WILL**
manumitters exrtaordinaire

Contents

1.   **INTRODUCTION**   2

Organization of the essay, 8.

2.   **SOME NOTES ON SCIENTIFIC DEDUCTIVE SYSTEMS**   10

1. *Theories as Deductive Systems, 11.*   **2.** *Empirical Science and the Criterion of Falsification, 19.*   *Conclusions, 23.*

3.   **THE THEORY OF DEMAND**   26

1. *Utility Analysis, 28.*   **2.** *Theory of Revealed Preference, 42.*

4.   **THE FUNCTION OF CONCEPTS IN THE THEORY OF DEMAND**   46

1. *The Formation of Concepts in Science, 47.*   **2.** *Concepts and Definitions in the Theory of Demand, 53.*   *Conclusions, 62.*

5.   **THE FUNCTION OF LAWS IN THE THEORY OF DEMAND**   64

1. *The Function of General Laws in Explanation and Prediction, 65.* **2.** *Explanation and Prediction in the Theory of Demand, 72.*

6.   **THE ECONOMIST'S DILEMMA**   86

1. *Prediction as the Criterion of Empirical Validity, 87.*   **2.** *Other Approaches to Empirical Validation, 96.*

7.   **TOWARD A SET OF TESTABLE POSTULATES**   102

1. *On the Theory of Reduction, 104.*   **2.** *On Reduction and a Theory of Human Decision-Making, 109.*   *Conclusions, 118.*

8.   **TOWARD A TESTABLE THEORY OF DEMAND**   120

1. *Toward a Theory of Consumer Behavior, 122.*   **2.** *Interpreting the Proposed Theory, 133.*   **3.** *On Reducing the Theory of Demand, 136.*

9.   **SUMMARY AND CONCLUSIONS**   140

     BIBLIOGRAPHY   146

     INDEX   150

The Theory of Consumer Demand:
A Critical Appraisal

1

Introduction

The history of economic thought is in part a history of a dispute over the criteria to be employed when adjudging the validity of contending economic theories. Because of its fundamental importance to the development of a coherent body of theory, this debate has survived innumerable discussions and is in fact as vital an issue today as it was in the ruminations of early economists. As with many prolonged disceptations, there is a central piece of data that is as difficult to displace as to ignore. Consequently, it is the desire to dispose of or to accommodate the awkward data that stimulate and prolong the polemics.

In the economic debate we are concerned with, the datum is provided by the unpleasant but often noted fact that the predictive powers of economic theories are strikingly weak when compared to those of the physical sciences. Economists have responded to this irritant by developing and employing a set of criteria that largely ignore this lack of predictive success. As a result economic theories are normally judged on the basis of such criteria as their consistency with accepted doctrine, or their ability to be deduced from standard premises, all of which avoid any direct reference to empirical phenomena. This is certainly not to say that economists are uninterested in developing theories which explain and predict the course of economic events. It is rather that the notable poverty of predictive success has led them to adopt other criteria by which to appraise and reject contending theories.

If a theory is to be judged by alternative sets of criteria, then the choice of criteria can be expected to influence the way in which the theory is constructed. If consistency with accepted doctrine is the chief criterion, then one can readily predict that new theories will not be proposed that violate this constraint. Therefore, it is pertinent to inquire whether it is the criteria themselves, or the nature of the subject matter that has led economic theory into this unfortunate state of affairs. Both the existence and the intensity of the debate might lead one to suppose that most economists preferred the former to the latter answer to this question.[1] But this does not

---

[1] A recent example of this dispute, with references to some of its history, can be found in the *Southern Economic Journal*, Vol. **XXII**, July, 1955, in the paper by F. Machlup, "The Problem of Verification in Economics," pp. 1–21, the reply by T. W. Hutchison, "Professor Machlup on Verification in Economics," and Machlup's "Rejoinder to a Reluctant Ultra-Empiricist," pp. 476–493.

in fact appear to be the case. Instead many economists have argued that the absence of good predictions is due to the fact that economic theory, by its very nature, differs from the type of theory found in the physical sciences. In particular, it is frequently asserted that the problems of developing and testing economic theory are essentially different from those encountered in the physical sciences; and many ingenious and, at times, impressive arguments have been proposed in support of this claim.[2]

It is our opinion, however, that this position is mistaken, and that it is the criteria and not the subject matter that are at fault. Moreover, it is the principal purpose of this essay to demonstrate that the source of the affliction lies within the theories of economics themselves and not within the nature of the subject matter.

To suggest that the theories of economics are defective is to suggest that they have been constructed in a manner that does not permit successful predictions to be generated from them. Even though this may appear to be an obvious statement of the case, it clearly implies that economic theories must be unable to meet the standards normally applied to physical theories. In other words, if physical theories can be used to predict the course of physical events, then the criteria employed by physicists must differ from those employed by economists. If these two sets of criteria do in fact differ, then the observation that economic theory is not a part of empirical science would be sufficient to account for the notable lack of success economists have had in predicting the course of economic events. Yet to observe that economic theories do not belong within the pale of empirical science does not imply that they must forever remain in this state. On the contrary, to arrive at this conclusion is to provide the necessary first step along whatever program of revision and reform is required. To recognize the etiology of a disease is the first essential step towards prescribing its cure.

While we have no desire to belittle the difficulty of constructing theories that can successfully predict economic events, we are unable to accept the position that it is not possible to do so. Hence,

---

[2] An excellent review of the forms this argument has taken can be found in: S. Schoeffler, *The Failures of Economics: A Diagnostic Study*, Harvard University Press, 1955, Ch. 2.

the first part of this essay is devoted to securing our position by demonstrating the existence of this necessary first step. That is to say, we shall endeavor to establish and defend the following proposition: that the absence of successful predictions is due to the fact that the theories of economics are unable to meet the normal requirements employed in empirical science.

Unfortunately, the classes of economic theory are both many and disparate, and it is certainly beyond the scope of one essay to establish the validity of this proposition for *all* economic theories. To select one theory for extensive examination, however, might be construed as being unnecessarily arbitrary. Critics could rightfully protest that whatever might be true for one specific theory need not be true for the remainder. To circumvent the somewhat arbitrary nature of any choice we might make, we shall base our selection on one of the avowed objectives of economics itself—namely, to describe and predict the behavior of economic man. Accordingly, we have taken as the subject of our investigation the micro-economic theory of consumer behavior. From this decision, it follows that in the first part of this book we shall essay to establish the following propositions:

(i) that it is not possible to employ the micro-economic theory of consumer behavior (the theory of demand) to generate empirically significant predictions about consumer behavior.

(ii) that this predictive void is due to the fact that the theory of demand is unable to meet the normal requirements employed in empirical science.

To pose these propositions in this manner suggests that normative questions, historically of greater concern to economists, have become less important. We have, however, no desire to disparage either the importance or the success economists have had in developing and applying some normative theories. We only insist that it is the positive (or descriptive) theories that provide the scientific basis for policy prescriptions. If some positive theories cannot be empirically confirmed, then it must follow that their normative counterparts have no scientific foundation, and that such policy prescriptions as are derived from them are devoid of empirical relevance. Admittedly this is by no means the first time it has been suggested that some of the principal theories of economics cannot be corroborated by empirical test,[3] but the implications of this assertion are sufficiently serious to warrant a searching examination of the truth of this claim. Furthermore, in the normal course of events it may not occur to economists to question the empirical validity of their principal theories. However, once the question has been raised and their validity challenged, it is not sufficient merely to ascertain whether these theories can meet one set of criteria or not. After all, it can be readily argued that there are many ways in which a given body of theory may be used, as well as many different sets of criteria by which a particular theoretical construction may be judged. Therefore, before we can begin our investigation we must in some sense justify the criteria that we are going to employ.

As noted above the motivation for this study is provided by a desire to demonstrate that the lack of predictability in economic theories does not stem from any inherent difficulties in the subject matter itself. The difficulties arise from the fact that the theories of economics have failed to meet the standards governing empirical science. We are clearly assuming, therefore, that it is highly desirable that economic theories, whether they currently do meet these standards or not, should be constructed so that they can be accepted as a part of empirical science. From the discussion of this point in the literature it appears that many economists do not agree with this position, but the acceptance of this goal implies that the criteria by which we should judge the theory of demand are those which are generally accepted as the criteria for the demarcation of empirical science.

Although we have no desire to compete with philosophers of science, both the reader as well as the author must be agreed on the uses and meanings of the terms that are to be employed in this study. Thus, even though economists almost invariably disapprove of methodological discussions, allowances must be made if we are to describe the analytical tools we shall employ.

To those who share our basic views our proposed investigation

---

[3] For examples of other authors who have asserted that the theories of economics are largely devoid of empirical content see: T. W. Hutchison, *The Significance and Basic Postulates of Economic Theory*, Macmillan and Company, London, 1938; and A. G. Papandreou, *Economics as a Science*, Lippincott Co., New York, 1958.

of part of micro-economic theory is perhaps a laudable task by itself. Yet the notable lack of predictive success this body of theory has encountered would *prima facie* tend to indicate that it would not meet the criteria governing empirical science. To carry out this indagation only to conclude that the theory of demand does not meet the same standards that are met by some physical theories would not appear, by itself, to be a particularly significant contribution to our knowledge. What would be important, though, is to use this analysis to discover the ways in which these two types of theories differ, and, as a result, to isolate and identify those factors that have kept economics from becoming a part of science.

But to point out the stumbling blocks is only to expose oneself to the greatest temptation of all—namely, the immodest desire to suggest a possible solution to the dilemma. Once the quarry has been identified and the first signs of a trail have been exposed it is very difficult not to press on. The second half of this essay, therefore, is devoted to the task of proposing a solution to this predicament. In brief, we shall outline one possible way in which the theory of demand can be rescued from the mere fringes of empirical science and turned into a testable theory of consumer behavior. In doing so we shall take pains to outline and support each step of our proposed solution with such evidence as we can muster. It is of course understood that our approach to the resolution of the difficulty is not the only possible one. We only hope that if one solution can be proposed and worked out, then other and more effective procedures for achieving the same results can be discovered. It is in this spirit that the second half of this essay is written.

The final purpose of this study then is not to increase by one the number of articles and books written on the problems of verification in economics. Rather our object is of a much more positive kind. Our goal is to refute the proposition that the development and testing of economic theory is essentially different from that encountered in the physical sciences by proposing and demonstrating the validity of the following two propositions:

(i) that the problems of developing and testing micro-economic theory need be no different from those encountered in the physical sciences.

(ii) that it is possible to develop a body of micro-economic theory having the same explanatory and predictive power as is enjoyed by the physical sciences.

Thus, while this essay will only be concerned with the theory of demand we are suggesting that the implications of our analysis apply to the entire body of micro-economic theory.

ORGANIZATION OF THE ESSAY

As we mentioned earlier, the history of economic thought is replete with discussions on the criteria that should be employed when judging the validity of economic theory. Since we are proposing that economics should be judged by the standards employed in empirical science, it is necessary to define and describe what these standards entail. The next chapter, therefore, is devoted to a discussion of some of the fundamental terms and analytical tools that we will employ throughout the book. Before we can begin our analysis, however, we must be agreed upon the content of the theory that we are going to examine. Consequently, in Chapter 3 we present the essential parts of the theory of demand as it is currently received. So that our analysis may proceed in an orderly fashion, our next concern is to examine the concepts of the theory in order to identify their sources of empirical content. This analysis is presented in Chapter 4. We then turn in Chapter 5 to an investigation of the function of the theory's postulates and laws in the explanation and prediction of an economic event. In Chapter 6 we present the results of our investigation and isolate and identify what we have taken the liberty of calling the "economist's dilemma." Having reached our necessary first step, Chapters 7 and 8 are then devoted to outlining what we consider to be both a possible and a practical solution to the problem of developing an empirically testable theory of demand. The last chapter contains a summary of what we have set out to accomplish and the conclusions that the results appear to warrant.

Some Notes on Scientific
Deductive Systems

"Empirical science, in all its major branches, seeks not only to DESCRIBE *the phenomena in the world of our experience, but also to* EXPLAIN *or* UNDERSTAND *their occurrences: it is concerned not just with the 'What?', 'When?', and 'Where?', but definitely and predominantly with the 'Why?' of the phenomena it investigates."*[1]

From this definition it appears that not every theory we might see fit to construct to "explain" a particular set of observations would be classified as belonging to the body of empirical science. Some of our theories, e.g., theories about the behavior of historical personages, might only contain a description of the events under consideration. In this case there would be an implicit understanding that we would be able to "explain" the occurrence of a new event if the description of this further event coincided with the description in our theory. On the other hand, we might have constructed a general theory which appeared to "fit" or "explain" a large number of individual cases, e.g. a regression line drawn through a particular sample of data, but from which we could not with any assurance of success predict the "What?", "When?" or "Where?" of the next relevant case. Because somehow the theories of empirical science are supposed to combine all of these elements, it is the purpose of this chapter to examine some of the basic criteria a theory must meet if it is to be classified as belonging to the corpus of empirical science.

1. THEORIES AS DEDUCTIVE SYSTEMS

From this brief discussion it is apparent that one of the main functions of a scientific theory is to "explain" the "Why?" of the phenomena it investigates. It is also evident that to be able to answer the "Why?" of an event is not perhaps as easy as it may appear. One of the conditions that must be met is that the phenomena to be "explained" must be inferable from the theoretical structure. That is to say, the occurrence of the event to be

---

[1] Carl G. Hempel, "The Logic of Functional Analysis," in L. Gross (ed.) *Symposium on Sociological Theory*, Row, Peterson and Company, New York, 1959, p. 271.

"explained" must be deducible as a direct consequence from the concatenation of the theory and some initial conditions. For this condition to be met the theoretical system must conform to the general rules of logic that govern the formation and manipulation of deductive systems. Thus, in order to examine the nature of a scientific theory we must first examine some of the principal characteristics of deductive systems.

A. Deductive Systems as a Calculus

Everyone who has ever had to learn some simple mathematics or geometry knows that the essence of a deductive system consists in a process of deriving a desired set of propositions (frequently called theorems) from a given, initial set of propositions (frequently called axioms). The derivation of the desired proposition is achieved by following a set of rules that enables us to derive a variety of new propositions from the original set. By repeated application of the same rules we eventually arrive at a statement of the desired proposition. While the content of these propositions may pertain to any body of knowledge whatsoever, it is the formal structure of the deductive system—that is, the set of rules—that we are concerned with here.

In order to examine the properties of a deductive system we first need a technique of representing and classifying the concomitant set of rules or deductive principles. Fortunately, the logician has provided us with the required analytical tools. Within this analytic framework deductive principles are represented by a set of symbolic rules which govern the manipulation of abstract symbols. A particular collection of these symbolic rules is called a calculus. Accordingly, we can distinguish a deductive system from the calculus that represents its formal structure in the following way: An inquiry into the properties of a calculus belongs to what is called syntax or syntactics; while an inquiry into the relation between a calculus and the deductive system it represents belongs to semantics.[2] Since it is usually easier and sometimes more fruitful

---

[2] For a more detailed discussion of these concepts and terms see: R. Carnap, "Foundations of Logic and Mathematics," *International Encyclopedia of Unified Science*, University of Chicago Press, Vol. I, No. 3, 1939.

to give examples of a concept rather than to rigorously define it, we shall dwell only briefly on the formal properties of a calculus before providing an example.

A calculus, considered by itself, is a set of rules that allows an operator to manipulate a given set of symbols in such a way that he can transform one series of symbols into another. The symbols themselves may belong to a particular language, like English or mathematics, or they may merely be a collection of uninterpreted marks on a piece of paper. What distinguishes a calculus from a particular set of deductive principles written, say, in the English language is that the rules of the calculus specify how the manipulations are to be carried out without making any reference to the "meaning" of the symbols themselves. For this reason a calculus can be viewed as a symbolic game in which each move of the game is governed by the specified rules.

The components of a calculus can now be specified as follows: The vocabulary is defined by making a list of the symbols that are to be used. These symbols are the *primitive symbols* of the calculus and may represent, in a manner to be discussed later, the components of a deductive system. Primitive symbols can be strung together into sequences in a variety of ways. Any finite sequence of these symbols is called a formula. Nevertheless, since we are usually only interested in dealing with formulas that have specified properties, a set of rules is required that will determine which are the permissible or *well-formed formulas*. A calculus, therefore, must contain a set of formation rules as well as a set of primitive symbols.

Before we can begin to manipulate symbols and formulas we must have somewhere to start from. In a calculus the initial position is determined by selecting a specific set of well-formed formulas. These formulas are identified as the axioms for the system, and are accepted as the basic formulas of the calculus game.

In order to employ these axioms to generate new formulas we need to have some rules of play. In a calculus these rules are provided by a set of *rules of inference*. Rules of inference (or rules of procedure) specify the types of manipulation that are to be allowed. By applying these rules to the axioms we can infer or generate other well-formed formulas. And, if we have as the object of our manipulations the derivation of a particular formula, we can employ the rules of inference to see whether this particular formula can be inferred from the axioms we have selected. It should be noted that there is nothing within the rules of the calculus itself to guarantee that we can infer a particular well-formed formula from a given set of axioms. On the contrary, the choice of a particular sequence of inferences, just like a choice of a particular sequence of moves in a game, is up to the player. The calculus merely specifies the procedures by which the formulas are to be inferred.

Once a particular well-formed formula has been arrived at by a specific sequence of inferences from one or more of the axioms, this sequence of formulas is called a *proof* of the last formula in the sequence. Once a proof has been discovered for a particular formula, this formula is usually called a theorem to distinguish it from other well-formed formulas for which no proof has yet been constructed.

So far our calculus contains primitive symbols, formation rules, axioms, rules of inference, and a definition of what constitutes a proof. If there were no other prerequisites, it is clear that we could construct a calculus in an infinite variety of ways. We would be free to choose our symbols, rules of formation, and rules of inference in any manner we thought convenient at the time. To do so, however, might lead us to build systems of calculi in which proofs could be established for self-contradictory and other inappropriate types of formulas. For this reason, a calculus is required to meet the condition of *consistency*. Once we have a consistent system the only other requirements to be met are that the calculus be *complete* and that its axioms be independent. Although these concepts are too complex to be discussed here in any detail, their properties can be roughly characterized as follows:

A consistent calculus is one in which not every well-formed formula is a theorem. In the case where the calculus includes the notion of negation, this notion implies that a calculus is inconsistent if a specific well-formed formula and its negation are both provable within the system. The concept of completeness, on the other hand, requires that every well-formed formula *or* its negation be a theorem of the system. That is to say, if a calculus is complete, and if a well-formed formula which is *not* a theorem is added to the system, this addition would make the calculus inconsistent. Finally, the independence requirement is met if it can be shown that the axioms of a calculus cannot be inferred one from another. As a result, the axioms of a calculus are independent if it can be shown that by deleting any one of them, the remaining axioms are not sufficient to establish a proof of the one deleted.

Having briefly discussed the properties of a calculus, we shall now examine an example of such a system so as to demonstrate its analytical uses in investigating the properties of a scientific theory. The example we shall use is taken from the class of calculi known as the *propositional or sentential calculus*. Before we can go on to the example we must first make clear the distinction between: the language that is under examination, the *object* language, and the language we use to talk about the object language, the *metalanguage*.

The need for this distinction should be readily apparent. For example, a student taking a course in physics deals with the language of physics as his object language and employs his spoken language, English in this instance, as his metalanguage. The physical symbols of the object language have no meaning until they are interpreted by means of the metalanguage. However, once the symbols in the object language have been assigned a meaning, then the physical theory has become a deductive system with which the student can now make meaningful manipulations.

In our example, therefore, the calculus consists of two kinds of marks. The first are a series of capital letters, e.g. 'A', 'B', 'C', 'D', whose number can be expanded by the use of subscripts, e.g. 'A_1', 'B_1', 'C_1', 'D_1', 'A_2', 'B_2', 'C_2', 'D_2', . . . The second kind consists of four marks: '$\sim$', '$\supset$', '((', and '))'. All of these symbols belong to the object language of this calculus, and if we are to be able to talk about these marks in a metalanguage we need to have some names for them. Hence, in our metalanguage the name of a capital letter will be given by the same letter italicized, e.g. the name of 'A' is 'A', the name of 'B' is 'B', etc. Also the names of the other four marks, '$\sim$', '$\supset$', '))', '((' are '$\sim$', '$\rightarrow$', '$)$', '$($' respectively.

Now the letters 'A', 'B', 'C', 'D' are formulas or statements in the object language; and if we are to be able to talk in the metalanguage about the formulas of the object language we need one further set of marks. These marks in the metalanguage are 'P', 'Q', 'R', 'S'. They are called *variables* and may be used in the metalanguage to denote any well-formed formula in the object language.

Therefore, if the formation rules are such that P, $\sim P$, $P \rightarrow Q$, $\sim P \rightarrow \sim Q$, and $\sim(P \rightarrow Q)$[3] are all well-formed formulas, it is easy to see how we can begin to construct statements or formulas in the metalanguage. In order to carry out some manipulations with these formulas we employ two rules of inference. The first, called *modus ponens*, states that if we are given the formula P and the formula $P \rightarrow Q$, then we can infer the formula Q. Hence, the rule of *modus ponens* allows us to draw the conclusion Q from the major premiss $P \rightarrow Q$ and the minor premiss P. The second rule, called the *rule of substitution*, permits us to substitute one variable for another within a formula as long as this substitution is carried out for each occurrence of the variable in question. For example, if we were given the formula $P \rightarrow Q$, this rule allows us to substitute R for P and S for Q and get the formula $R \rightarrow S$. Hence, if we were given the formula $P \rightarrow (Q \rightarrow P)$, as an axiom, and were asked to construct a proof of the formula $S \rightarrow (R \rightarrow S)$, we could proceed in the following way. We would note that if we substituted S for P and R for Q that we could apply the rule of substitution and immediately arrive at the formula $S \rightarrow (R \rightarrow S)$. Thus, the proof would consist of a single application of the substitution rule.

If we now wanted to write down a proof for the formula $(R \rightarrow S)$ we would previously need to be able to construct a proof for S. That is to say, since we already have a proof for $S \rightarrow (R \rightarrow S)$, if we could construct a proof for S, then by the rule of *modus ponens* we could infer $(R \rightarrow S)$. To be able to continue to develop proofs for various formulas in this calculus we only need have an independent set of axioms and the assurance that our system was both consistent and complete. For our purposes we are only interested in presenting the calculus as a tool for analyzing deductive systems, and we shall not develop our example any further.[4] Instead we shall now examine the problem of interpreting these systems.

---

[3] Throughout the remainder of the book the single quotation marks ' ' will be omitted; and the reader is requested either to imagine that they are there, or to supply them himself.

[4] This system of propositional calculus is presented in its entirety in: A. Church, *Introduction to Mathematical Logic*, Princeton University Press, 1956, Vol. 1, Ch. II.

B. *Interpreting the Calculus*

Up to now we have presented the calculus as a system consisting of symbols, formation rules, and rules of inference or manipulation. Before we can apply our calculus to a particular context, we need to have some rules whereby we can interpret the meaning of the symbols as well as the meaning of the well-formed formulas of which these symbols are a part. Not only do we need to know what the particular symbols represent, but we also need to be able to tell what it is that is being asserted by any particular statement or formula. In short we need an effective procedure for determining the meaning of the well-formed formulas that can be generated within a deductive system. First, however, we need to assign an interpretation to the statements in our calculus. In this case we shall let A, B, C, D be the names of statements in the calculus, and let the calculus be composed of English sentences. Hence, P, Q, R, S, which are variables in the metalanguage, will denote any of the English sentences contained in the calculus. So as to simplify the analysis as much as possible, these statements will be restricted to simple sentences such as 'this wire is made of copper' and 'this wire conducts electricity'. To complete the interpretation we need to give a meaning to the two connectives $\rightarrow$ and $\sim$. That is to say, we should have a procedure for determining exactly what is being asserted by the statement 'this wire is made of copper' $\rightarrow$ 'this wire conducts electricity'.

To each statement such as 'this wire is made of copper' we can assign a *truth value*–that is, the statement must either have the value 'true' or 'false'. Consequently, if we take two such statements and link them together by the connective $\rightarrow$, e.g. 'this wire is made of copper' $\rightarrow$ 'this wire conducts electricity', then we will know what is being asserted by this statement if we know the conditions under which the expression has the value 'true' and those under which its value is 'false'. A solution to this problem is provided by what are called truth tables. Truth tables specify the truth value for a statement for the different combinations of truth values of its component parts. For example, the truth table for '$\rightarrow$' is given by Table (i) while the truth table for '$\sim$' is given by Table (ii).

From Tables (i) and (ii) it is apparent that we have made the symbol '$\rightarrow$' correspond to the English words 'if . . . then' or

Table (i)

P Q	$P \rightarrow Q$
T T	T
T F	F
F T	T
F F	T

Table (ii)

P	$\sim P$
T	F
F	T

'implies', and the symbol '$\sim$' correspond to the English word 'not'. Also from Table (i) we can see that if we know the value of P is 'true' and that of Q is 'false', then the value of the statement $P \rightarrow Q$ is 'false'. Indeed, it should be noted that this is the *only* set of truth values that will give the value 'false' to the proposition $P \rightarrow Q$. Clearly, we can also use this table to find out the truth value of the formula we took as an axiom for our recent example—namely, $P \rightarrow (Q \rightarrow P)$. In this case we find that no matter what values we ascribe to P and Q the value of the formula is always 'true'. For example, let the value of P be 'false' and that of Q be 'true'. To derive the truth value of the whole statement we first consider the part within the parentheses, i.e. $(Q \rightarrow P)$. From the table we conclude that its value is 'false'. Hence, the values of P and $(Q \rightarrow P)$ are both 'false', and it follows that the value of $P \rightarrow (Q \rightarrow P)$ is 'true'. In a similar manner we could compute the value of this relation for the other values of P and Q. A few calculations will quickly show that the value of $P \rightarrow (Q \rightarrow P)$ is always 'true'. Thus, we can conclude that the truth value of this expression is independent of the truth value of its component parts. If the truth value of a statement is independent of the truth value of its component parts then its value must depend on the truth value given to it by its logical connectives. Statements of this sort are called tautologies, and are described as being logically true—that is, their value is 'true' independent of the values ascribed to their individual parts.

If all the statements in our deductive system are tautologies then it is called a "pure"[5] deductive system. Needless to say, not all deductive systems are pure deductive systems. The procedure, therefore, for determining the truth value of a particular statement

---

[5] The terms "pure" and "applied" are taken from R. B. Braithwaite, *Scientific Explanation*, Cambridge University Press, 1953, p. 34.

differs depending on whether the deductive system can be classified as being pure or not. As we have seen, in a pure deductive system the truth value of both the initial and of the inferred statements depends solely upon their logical connectives. In the case of an applied deductive system, the truth value of a sentence does not depend solely upon the truth value of its logical connectives, but instead upon whether its component parts are suitably supported by the available empirical evidence. Since empirical science is composed of various types of applied deductive systems, the following sections are devoted to examining the problems that arise in determining the truth values of the statements that appear in these systems.

2. EMPIRICAL SCIENCE AND THE CRITERION OF FALSIFICATION

In the previous section we noted that a deductive system could be characterized by its underlying calculus. While both the pure and the applied deductive systems are alike in this respect, they differ in the procedures that are used to establish the truth value of their respective propositions. Since empirical science can be characterized as an applied deductive system, a procedure that establishes the truth value of a relation in an applied system must also be a procedure that determines the truth values of propositions in empirical science. Thus, our examination of the truth values of an applied deductive system is also an examination of the way in which truth values can be established for the postulates and hypotheses of an empirical science.

In order to present this analysis in an orderly fashion, we shall first take up the problem of determining the truth value for a simple contingent proposition,[6] whose component parts depend for their truth values upon the available empirical evidence.

To carry out this analysis we shall make use of the following example: In the previous section we saw that the variables P, Q, R, S could represent English sentences. Also that the proposition $P \rightarrow Q$ could represent the statement: If 'this wire is made of

---

[6] For a more detailed examination of the roles of contingent propositions in deductive systems see: R. B. Braithwaite, *op. cit.* pp. 34 ff.

copper' then 'this wire conducts electricity'. Now suppose for the moment that we are anxious to find out whether this statement is "empirically true."[7] Before we can answer this question we must first know what data are required to confirm this hypothesis. To answer this question we must return for a moment to the truth tables to examine the conditions under which this hypothesis can be confirmed.

From the truth tables we observe that if the antecedent clause 'this wire is made of copper' has the value 'true', then the value of the expression will depend on the truth value of the consequent 'this wire conducts electricity'. In all the remaining cases, e.g. when the value of the antecedent is 'false', the truth value of the expression is 'true' whether the consequent has the value 'true' or not. Hence, if we wish to confirm the expression, we must first know whether or not the antecedent is supported by the empirical evidence. If the evidence does not support the statement 'this wire is made of copper', then we cannot submit the expression to an empirical test. On the other hand, if we have data that support the statement 'this wire is made of copper' then the expression $P \rightarrow Q$ will be confirmed if we can find empirical support for the consequent Q. In other words, the only way we can tell whether $P \rightarrow Q$ is empirically true is to observe both that 'this wire is made of copper' and that 'this wire conducts electricity'. In this case we can state that the expression has been empirically confirmed.

If, however, we had stated this expression in a more general form—namely, 'all wires that are made of copper conduct electricity'—then it is clear that while confirming instances can still be found, we shall never be able to tell whether this expression will always be supported by the data. Thus the minute we extend the singular statement $P \rightarrow Q$ into the general statement 'all instances of P are also instances of Q' it follows that we can no longer

---

[7] In the remainder of this essay the term "empirically true" will be considered equivalent to the term "empirically confirmed". By these terms we mean that the available evidence supports the hypothesized expression. This by no means implies that the expression has somehow been empirically "proved". On the contrary, the best that can be said is that the evidence does not contradict the hypothesis. Thus, in all cases where these terms are used we will be using them as an abbreviation for the statement, "the evidence has not yet disconfirmed the expression."

hope to be able to completely determine its truth value. Instead we can only determine for each set of observations whether the statement has been confirmed or not.

The problem of determining the truth value of an expression becomes even more involved if we introduce into our applied deductive systems propositions that contain one or more terms for which no empirical evidence can be directly gathered, i.e. non-observational terms. Under these conditions it is no longer possible to determine whether the expression has been confirmed or not. For example, let the variable P represent the statement A which in turn contains a term that is not definable in observational terms. Let Q represent the statement B whose terms are all observationally defined. Then, if we wish to determine whether the statement $P \rightarrow Q$ is empirically true it does not help us to be able to tell that statement Q is supported by the empirical evidence. For whenever the value of Q is 'true', the value of the expression $P \rightarrow Q$ is also 'true' even though the statement P may be 'false'. Accordingly, if it is not possible to determine empirically the truth value of P, it is not possible to submit $P \rightarrow Q$ to a direct empirical test. As a result, the inclusion of non-observational concepts in the propositions of applied deductive systems makes it even more difficult to determine their empirical truth value.

Nevertheless, empirical science is concerned with developing bodies of theory that are empirically testable, even though its theories frequently contain non-observational concepts or terms, e.g., electrons, protons, atoms, etc. For this reason we cannot expect to find direct supporting evidence for all the terms in all the expressions of which a particular theory is composed. Because we can conclude that it is not always possible to directly confirm a particular theory, we must search for another criterion if we wish to be able to separate testable from non-testable theories.

A solution to this dilemma can be reached by approaching the problem from the opposite direction. In particular, a criterion of falsification can be employed.[8] This criterion states that a theory

---

[8] The criterion of falsifiability was developed by Karl Popper who asserts that a theory is a part of science if and only if it is possible to subject the theory to a process of refutation by empirical test. For an extensive discussion of this criterion see: Karl R. Popper, *The Logic of Scientific Discovery*, Basic Books, New York, 1959.

can be accepted as a part of empirical science if and only if it is possible to refute or disconfirm it by empirical test. This means that a theory can only be refuted if it asserts the existence of a set of data or expressions which contain observational terms. This criterion thus distinguishes between theories that do and theories that do not have empirically testable implications, and it classifies only the former as belonging to empirical science.

From our previous analysis it should be apparent that to be able to disconfirm a single hypothesis one must know that the value of the antecedent is 'true'. For example, to be able to disconfirm the hypothesis if 'this wire is made of copper' then 'this wire conducts electricity' we must first observe that the wire is made of copper before it is fruitful to examine whether the wire conducts electricity. If we cannot find out empirically whether the wire is made of copper then it is not possible to refute the expression $P \rightarrow Q$. Thus, if we employ the falsifiability criterion, a theory is not considered to be a part of empirical science unless it is possible to refute it by the appropriate empirical test.

To accept this criterion, however, does not dispose of the question of how to determine the empirical truth value of hypotheses that contain non-observational or theoretical terms. Some theorists have strongly urged that all such hypotheses should be restated so that they only contain observational terms.[9] Unfortunately, such a position would seriously undermine a number of very important theoretical structures. If, however, we do not agree to dispose of all non-observational terms, then we do need a set of procedures that enables us to determine whether such a theory can be considered empirically testable.

In practice this problem is resolved by requiring a theory to provide some deduced hypotheses that are themselves capable of

---

[9] This methodological position, entitled "operationism," was first advanced by P. W. Bridgman in *The Logic of Modern Physics*, Macmillan, New York, 1927. For an excellent survey of the adequacy and applicability of this technique see: "Symposium on Operationism," *Psychological Review*, Vol. **52**, Sept., 1955, especially the contribution by H. Feigl, "Operationism and Scientific Method," pp. 250–259. For a more recent analysis of the problems posed by the operationist's approach see: Carl G. Hempel, "The Theoretician's Dilemma," *Minnesota Studies in the Philosophy of Science*, University of Minnesota, 1958, Vol. **II**, pp. 37–98.

being refuted by empirical test. In other words if a theory is to be considered to be empirically testable it must be possible to deduce from it a set of expressions that only contain observational terms. If such is not the case—that is, if it is not possible to deduce from the theory a set of expressions that are refutable by empirical test— then there is no way of determining the empirical truth value of the theory. As a result we do not have an effective procedure for ensuring that the theory has been empirically confirmed. The application of the criterion of falsifiability, however, does provide us with a set of procedures whereby it is possible to determine whether the truth value of a given body of theory can be subjected to a series of empirical tests.[10]

CONCLUSIONS

At the beginning of this chapter we noted that the principal objective of empirical science is to "explain" the "Why?" of the phenomena it investigates. Although an examination of what is meant by the term "explain" is left until later in the text,[11] what we have been concerned with is an examination of the basic structure of a scientific theory. In our discussion we noted that a deductive system can be represented by a calculus which in turn must be interpreted if it is to represent an applied or an empirical deductive system. We also noted that it was necessary to have a decision rule with which to determine the truth value of the formulas or statements contained in the system. While an effective procedure was described for determining the logical truth value of a given statement, a number of problems were encountered when we tried to establish an effective procedure for determining their empirical truth value. Consequently, we had to adopt a set of procedures that do not guarantee the empirical truth value of a given body of theory, although they do permit us to determine whether it is possible to test for its empirical truth value. For this reason, we

---

[10] This issue is discussed in much greater detail by Carl G. Hempel, "Problems and Changes in the Empiricist Criterion of Meaning," *Revue Internationale de Philosophie*, Vol. 11, 1950. (Reprinted in L. Linsky (ed.), *Semantics and the Philosophy of Language*, University of Illinois Press, 1954.
[11] See Chapter 5.

cannot hope to be able to decide, for example, whether the theory of demand is empirically true or not. The best that we shall be able to do is to inspect the theory to see whether it is possible to submit it to a process of refutation by empirical test.

In our previous analysis we observed that if the concepts of a set of expressions are non-observational—that is, have no direct empirical content—then it is not possible to directly submit these expressions to empirical tests. Needless to say, if all the concepts of a deductive system are devoid of empirical content, then it is not possible to submit the theoretical structure to an empirical test. Because this is seldom the case, we shall first examine the theory of demand to determine the sources and the extent of the empirical content of its concepts and terms. Having examined the concepts and terms we shall then inspect the postulates and hypotheses to see whether any or all of them can be submitted to a process of refutation by empirical test. If some of the concepts have sufficient empirical content so that some of the hypotheses contain testable statements, then it is possible to submit at least part of the theory to empirical test. In this event, the theory as a whole must then be considered a part of empirical science. Conversely, if the theory does not contain any such hypotheses, then it follows that we cannot consider it a part of empirical science. Consequently, when we examine the hypothesized relations in the theory of demand, our principal concern shall be to decide whether these relations have sufficient empirical interpretation to allow their truth values to be determined by the appropriate empirical test.

In order to carry out this investigation we need to have before us the concepts and statements of which the theory of demand is composed. In spite of, perhaps, even because of the large number of books and articles that have been written on the subject, disagreement is too widespread to state precisely how the theory is to be interpreted. Our presentation will only be possible if we can agree, for the purposes of this essay, on the essential components of the theory. Therefore, even though the reader is undoubtedly familiar with at least one formulation of the theory of demand, the next chapter will be devoted to an explication of what we consider to be a reasonable consensus of its more important elements.

The Theory of Demand

This chapter is concerned with the parts of the theory of consumer behavior that pertain to the micro-economic theory of demand. As a result, the discussion will center upon the two types of theories that in our opinion best characterize its current state of development. Our approach, however, makes no attempt at being exhaustive. Rather, we intend to include only as much of the current theory as is suited to the purpose at hand.

The theory of demand is a theory about the behavior of consumers in the market place. Its purpose is to explain the process by which consumers make choices from among the alternative commodities available to them at any one point in time. The consumer in this theory is thought of as an entity whose object is to maximize the satisfaction he can derive from selecting the best possible combination of commodities he can afford. Originally, it was postulated that the consumer was able to measure the comparative utilities of alternative bundles of commodities on a cardinal utility scale. With the inclusion of a principle of diminishing marginal utility it became possible to identify the particular colleclection of commodities that would yield the highest utility. Moreover, by incorporating into the theory the postulates of a cardinal utility function and a principle of diminishing marginal utility, it was possible to show that for any given consumer there was a unique collection of commodities which maximized his satisfaction or utility. From this result it was then shown that a further piece of theory could be constructed from which the Law of Demand could be directly deduced—namely, that a rise (fall) in the price of an article would decrease (increase) the amount purchased, other things being held constant.

Current theories,[1] however, have dropped both of these restrictive postulates. It was discovered that the essential conclusions could be deduced from much weaker postulates about behavior. Since there are several theories of consumer behavior, and since we are going to examine only two of them here, it is well to remember that the Law of Demand is the goal toward which each theory is directed, as well as being one of the principal conclusions that must

---

[1] For an excellent survey of current theories of consumer behavior see: J. M. Henderson and R. E. Quandt, *Microeconomic Theory*, McGraw-Hill, New York, 1958, Ch. 2 and the references cited therein.

be reached if the theory is to be accepted as a possible explanation of consumer behavior. Because this is one important conclusion all the theories have in common, we shall present each theory in its form as an explanation of the Law of Demand. This means that we shall pay somewhat less attention to some of the other conclusions that are also derivable from them. Because these theories differ both in their basic postulates and in their points of departure, we shall begin with an examination of the utility maximizing approach and consider the theory of revealed preference later.

1. UTILITY ANALYSIS

One of the fundamental notions connected with these explanations of consumer behavior is the concept of utility. Early economists such as Jevons, Walras, and Marshall postulated that the consumer was capable of assigning to each commodity or combination of commodities a number that represented in cardinal terms the amount of utility associated with that selection of goods. It was also postulated that the consumer was aware of all of his possible alternatives, and, furthermore, that after he had assigned particular utilities to each of the alternatives he would then select the combination which yielded him the highest utility. Further, it was also postulated that as additional units of the same commodity were consumed the utility derived from this extra consumption would diminish. This is the famous principle of diminishing marginal utility. From these postulates it could be deduced that the consumer would increase his purchases of commodities, subject to his budget constraints, up to the point where there no longer was a net gain in utility. It was a brief step to infer from these results that a fall in the price of a commodity would increase the quantity purchased, other things remaining the same. Accordingly the law of demand with its various properties had been successfully derived.

Current theory, however, has abandoned the postulate of cardinal utility and has replaced it by an ordinal utility function. In this case it is postulated that the consumer can rank order the alternatives that are presented to him in terms of his preferences. This ranking of preferences does not imply that the consumer can state to what extent he prefers A to B, but rather only that he does prefer A to B. However, before these preferences can be represented by a utility function the conditions of three further postulates must be met. The first is that for all possible pairs of alternatives X and Y, the consumer must be able to say whether he prefers X to Y, Y to X, or whether he is indifferent between them. The second postulate requires the consumer to be able to make up his mind about all these alternatives so that only one of the three possibilities is true for any pair of alternatives. The third postulate is even more restrictive in that it requires the consumer to be consistent in his allocation of preferences—namely, if he prefers X to Y and Y to Z, then he must prefer X to Z. This condition of transitivity must apply to all possible pairs of alternatives.

A. The Utility Function

Because the theory of utility is designed to provide us with a foundation for the law of demand, the utility function is defined in terms of a consumer's purchases during a specified period of time. There is no unique time interval over which the utility function should be defined. The period usually chosen is such that the consumer has sufficient time to derive utility from a wide variety of purchased commodities. Whatever period is chosen, however, it must be remembered that the utility function is defined with respect to consumption only during that particular time interval. To be able to extend the analysis over longer intervals, the consumer is postulated to repeat his analysis and calculations at the beginning of each period.

From this brief discussion we can now move on to consider some of the properties of the utility function. We shall proceed in the normal manner by starting with the simple case where the consumer's purchases are limited to two commodities. The utility function can then be represented by:

$$U = f(x, m)$$

where x and m are the quantities purchased by the consumer of the two commodities X and M. In other words the utility derived from the purchase of a specific quantity of X and M is given by the point (x, m); and the locus of all such combinations of X and M

that yield the same level of utility is represented by the function
$U = f(x, m)$.

If X and M represent two particular commodities, such as apples
and potatoes, this simplified case appears to be unnecessarily
restrictive. If on the other hand, we allow X to represent one
commodity, say apples, and M to represent a composite commodity
that includes all other commodities,[2] then the simplified case no
longer appears to be quite so restrictive. Nevertheless, by letting
the second commodity, M, stand for a composite commodity we do
not have as close an approximation to reality as we might have at
first thought, since there are two further properties of the utility
function which we have not yet pointed out. First of all, it is postulated that the utility function is continuous, i.e., there are an infi-
nitely large number of combinations of X and M that lie along the
utility surface. This postulate implies that if we were only considering apples and potatoes, then both commodities would have to be
divisible into indefinitely small parts. The second postulate maintains that the utility function has continuous first and second order
partial derivatives, i.e., the utility function is postulated to represent a smooth, unbroken curve. Thus, if we consider once again
the case where X and M represent apples and potatoes, then these
two postulates imply that it is reasonable to consider the case where
a consumer is deliberating whether to select another tiny slice of
apple or a further morsel of potato. However, by substituting a
composite commodity for M, which could be represented by money,
the situation is less difficult to imagine. For M can now be divided
into relatively small parts with respect to X. Thus, although the
postulates of a continuous utility function with continuous first and
second order partial derivatives still imply complete divisibility of
the two commodities, a suitable interpretation of these commodities
can be employed to serve as a rough approximation in the simplified
case under consideration.

Now a particular level of utility, say U_0, can be derived from a

---

[2] The composite commodity is defined here in a Hicksian sense—that is, it
includes all other commodities including savings so that the total amount spent
on X and M represents the consumer's total income for the period. The only
way the total income cannot be spent within a given time period is by a physical
destruction of parts of M before it has been spent. This type of action is
specifically ruled out.

large variety of combinations of X and M. That this is so can readily be seen from the properties of the utility function just discussed. In principle, since $U = f(x, m)$ is continuous, there are an infinite number of combinations of X and M that will yield a certain amount of utility, say U_0. Further it is postulated that for a given amount of income the consumer will prefer combinations of commodities that yield greater rather than less utility. As a result, it is also a consequence of these postulates that the consumer is indifferent to choices between different combinations of goods that yield the same utility. It follows, therefore, that the consumer is, in principle, indifferent between the large variety of combinations

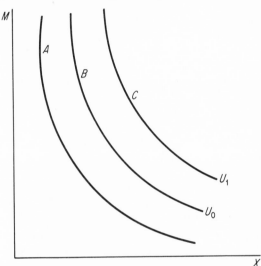

Figure 1.

of X and M that will yield the one level of utility given by U_0. The locus of points made by these combinations produces a curve known as the *Indifference Curve*. Hence, each indifference curve represents a particular level of utility. So that if a combination of X and M, given by (x_1, m_1) represents a level of utility U_1 which is greater than U_0, then the indifference curve representing U_1 will be placed above the curve representing U_0. Similarly, indifference curves that represent a level of utility lower than U_0 will be placed beneath U_0. For example, in Figure 1 if we let point $B = U_0$, then, by the way the indifference curves are placed, we can conclude the level of utility represented by point C is greater than that of A. In other words, if all other factors remain the same, the consumer would want to consume at the level given by C rather than at the levels given by B or A.

Even though the indifference curves in Figure 1 are drawn with negative slopes, nothing that we have covered in the preceding analysis justifies drawing them this way. That they should be negatively sloped is a very important deduction to be able to make, and it is toward this result that we now wish to proceed.

The slope of the indifference curve represents the rate at which the consumer is willing to substitute X for M, or M for X, in order to maintain a given level of utility. Our first task, therefore, is to see whether we can deduce what this rate of substitution is. To determine this rate of substitution we take the total differential of the utility function. This operation gives us the following equation:

$$dU = f_1\, dx + f_2\, dm \tag{3.1}$$

where f_1 and f_2 are the partial derivatives of U with respect to x and m respectively. But, as noted above, the indifference curve is defined as the locus of all points having the same utility, i.e., U is a constant. Therefore, by taking an arbitrary level of utility, say U_0, and substituting it into the Equation (3.1) we get:

$$0 = f_1\, dx + f_2\, dm, \tag{3.2}$$

and by transposing the terms (3.2) can be expressed by:

$$-\frac{dm}{dx} = \frac{f_1}{f_2}. \tag{3.3}$$

Thus the slope of the indifference curve, or the rate at which the consumer would be willing to substitute a certain amount of X for M, or M for X, is given by $-dm/dx$. The slope of the indifference curve in turn equals the ratio of the partial differentials of U with respect to x and m. So that if we could measure the quantities $f_1\, dx$ and $f_2\, dm$ we could directly determine the rate of substitution. However, we are dealing with an ordinal not a cardinal utility function. Consequently, these magnitudes cannot be measured directly. Nevertheless, by examining the rate of substitution of X for M, or M for X, we have shown that if f_1 and f_2 are positive, then the indifference curve has a negative slope—that is, the slope given by the ratio $-dm/dx$ has a negative sign in front of it. Unfortunately, we have not been able to measure what this slope is. To solve this, latter problem we must examine the conditions for equilibrium, or, in what amounts to the same thing, discover the particular combination of X and M that is sufficient to maximize a specific utility function.

To answer this question we must remember it has been postulated as part of this theory, that the consumer desires to purchase the specific combination of X and M from which he derives the highest level of utility. The highest level of utility a consumer can obtain is clearly the combination of X and M which, subject to his budget constraint, places him on the highest indifference curve. Thus, in order to specify the point at which the consumer obtains his greatest utility, we need to find the combination of X and M that maximizes his utility function subject to his budget constraint.

For any particular time period, the consumer's budget can be represented by

$$y^0 = p_x x + p_m m \qquad (3.4)$$

where y^0 represents the consumer's total income for this period, and p_x and p_m are the prices of X and M respectively. Because X and M include all possible ways for the consumer to spend his income, the amount spent on X, $(p_x x)$, plus the amount spent on M, $(p_m m)$, must equal his total income y^0.[3]

In order to maximize the utility function subject to the budget constraint we need to identify the combination of commodities that maximizes $U = f(x, m)$, while at the same time satisfying the budget equation $y^0 = p_x x + p_m m$. Since we have two equations in two unknowns, the task is quite straightforward. First, from the budget equation we get everything in terms of the commodity x. Transposing $p_m m$ to the left hand side, dividing through by p_x, and then transposing the left and right hand sides we have

$$x = \frac{y_0 - p_m m}{p_x}.$$

In other words, the amount purchased of commodity X, given by x, is equal to the consumer's total income for this period, y_0, minus the total amount he spends on M, $p_m m$, all of which is then divided by the price of X, given by p_x. By a straightforward substitution

---

[3] The reader will remember that we have chosen X to represent a particular commodity, say apples, while M stands for all the other possible commodities on the market, which in turn can be denoted by money.

of this value for x into the utility function, $U = f(x, m)$, we then have the utility function stated in terms of m alone.

$$U = f\left(\frac{y_0 - p_m m}{p_x}, m\right) \qquad (3.5)$$

To find the combination of X and M that maximizes the consumer's utility all we need do now is to find the maximum of (3.5) with respect to m. Having found a maximum value for m, the maximum value of x is immediately found by substituting this value for m back into the budget equation (3.4), as we already know the prices of X and M, i.e., p_x and p_m.

Now sufficient conditions for a maximum are satisfied if $(dU/dm) = 0$ and $(d^2U/dm^2) < 0$. These are what are called the first and second order conditions, respectively. In order to derive the first order conditions we take the first derivative of (3.5) with respect to m, i.e., dU/dm, and set it equal to zero. Taking the first derivative of (3.5) with respect to m we have

$$\frac{dU}{dm} = \frac{d}{dm}\left(\frac{y_0 - p_m m}{p_x}\right) + \frac{d}{dm}(m).$$

If we let

$$\frac{d}{dm} = f_1 \quad \text{and} \quad \frac{d}{dm}(m) = f_2$$

then

$$\frac{dU}{dm} = f_1\left(\frac{y_0 - p_m m}{p_x}\right) + f_2.$$

But, y_0 is a constant, therefore this equation can be reduced to

$$\frac{dU}{dm} = f_1\left(-\frac{p_m}{p_x}\right) + f_2.$$

Setting this equation equal to zero we have:

$$0 = f_1\left(-\frac{p_m}{p_x}\right) + f_2.$$

By transposing f_2 to the left hand side of the equation and dividing through by f_1 we then have

$$\frac{f_2}{f_1} = \left(\frac{p_m}{p_x}\right) \qquad (3.6)$$

which is the first order condition for a maximum.

By inverting the ratios on both sides of (3.6) we have $f_1/f_2 = p_x/p_m$. But, from our earlier analysis (3.3) we also have the equation $f_1/f_2 = -dm/dx$. Thus, from the first order conditions for a maximum we can conclude that $p_x/p_m = -dm/dx$ (3.7). That is to say, we have been able to demonstrate that the ratio of the price of X to the price of M is equal to the slope of the indifference curve. Since prices are always taken to be positive, Equation (3.7) implies that the slope of the indifference curve, e.g. $(-dm/dx)$, is always negative. Thus, by employing the first order conditions for a maximum we have been able to show that it is correct to draw an indifference curve with a negative slope as was done in Figure 1. That this is an important conclusion to be able to draw is illustrated by the following example. Consider a particular consumer who selects during one interval of time a combination of X and M given by (x_1, m_1). During the next period of time he selects a different combination of commodities given by (x_2, m_2). Also suppose that the utility derived by this consumer from his purchase of (x_1, m_1) is the same as is derived from (x_2, m_2), so that $U_1 = f(x_1, m_1) = f(x_2, m_2)$. We also shall assume that the quantities of X and M selected have not remained constant during these two periods. Thus, from the negative slope of his indifference curve we can conclude that if he increased his purchases of X he must have decreased his purchases of M, and vice versa. Further, if his indifference curve was precisely determined, then we could also specify the decrease in the amount of M purchased needed to offset a specific increase in X.

If there is to be a single point representing a specific collection of commodities at which the consumer derives the greatest utility from his given income, then there must be a unique point at which the indifference curve and the budget equation coincide. This point is characterized by the point at which the budget line is tangent to the indifference curve. For this to occur the indifference curve must be convex from below (viewing the curve from the origin), and hence as represented in Figure 1. By an examination of the second order conditions for a maximum—namely, that $d^2U/dm^2 < 0$—and the previously determined slope of the indifference curve (3.3), it can be shown that this is in fact the case and that the indifference curves can be represented by the curves as shown in Figure 1.[4] Hence for a given income and a given set of prices the consumer can be shown to maximize his utility if and only if he selects the combination of X and M which is represented by the point of tangency between his indifference curve and his budget equation.

For example, in Figure 2 the line AB represents the budget equation

$$y_0 = p_x x + p_m m.$$

The intercepts A and B on the M and X axes are the points at which the consumer's total income is spent on either M or X

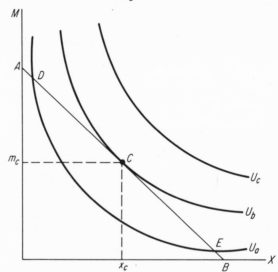

Figure 2.

respectively. The consumer is postulated to desire as high a level of utility as possible. Furthermore, as he cannot spend more than his income, the indifference curve he selects must intersect the line AB in at least one place. If the consumer decides to purchase the set of commodities represented by point D on AB, it is quite clear from the diagram that the utility he derives from this purchase, U_a, is less than the utility he would derive from purchasing the set of commodities represented by point C. Hence, since he can afford to purchase the commodities given by point C, the consumer will

---

[4] To be more precise, it can be shown that these indifference curves belong to a family of rectangular hyperbolas whose asymptotes coincide with the coordinate axes.

select that set of commodities, i.e. (x_c, m_c), and by this selection he will obtain the greatest utility from his purchases.

One further property of utility functions that can be inferred from the first and second order conditions is that this function is unique up to a monotonic transformation. This statement means that if, by a particular set of manipulations, we transform the utility function U into a new function $G(U)$, and if we also take two specific utility functions U_a and U_b where U_a represents a higher level of utility than U_b, then $G(U)$ is a monotonic transformation of U if when the same manipulations are applied to U_a and U_b, $G(U_a)$ always remains greater than $G(U_b)$. Another way of getting at the same point is to let U_a represent an index of utility. Then, as long as the consumer continues to maximize his utility subject to his budget constraint for a certain utility index, he will behave in an identical fashion no matter what utility index is chosen, so long as the new index is a monotonic transformation of the original one.

B. Demand Curves

The consumer's demand curve for a commodity is usually stated in terms of the quantity he will buy once the price is given. These curves are single-valued functions in prices and income. In the simple case we have been considering they can be represented by:

$$x = \frac{y^0}{2p_x} \quad \text{and} \quad m = \frac{y^0}{2p_m}.$$

These particular equations are derived directly from the equations representing the first order conditions of utility maximization. This derivation, however, imposes a constraint upon the interpretation of these demand curves. These curves can be derived only if the second order conditions for a maximum of utility are assumed to be true. That is to say, these curves can be inferred only if at the beginning of each new period the consumer continues to maximize his utility. As long as the consumer continues to maximize his utility we can see that once his income and the prices of X and M are known we can immediately infer the quantity of X and M he will purchase.

Two properties of these demand curves are worth noting: the first, as mentioned above, is that they are single-valued functions of prices and income. This property follows from the properties of the indifference curves we discussed earlier. The indifference curves are negatively sloped and are convex from below. Therefore, it follows that the point at which a consumer maximizes his utility corresponds to a single combination of commodities. This combination of commodities in turn corresponds to a particular set of prices and income. Thus, it can be directly inferred that as long as the consumer is maximizing his utility, his demand curves can be represented by a single valued function of prices and income.

The second property is that these demand functions can be shown to be homogeneous of zero*th* degree in both prices and income. This means that if all prices and income change in the same direction and in the same proportion, then the quantity demanded will remain the same. In terms of the more general demand function for X:

$$X = \phi(p_x, p_m, y^0),$$

this property implies that the consumer will not behave as though he were richer (or poorer) in terms of his real income if for the time period under discussion his actual income and the prices of X and M rise (or fall) in the same proportion.

With the consumer's demand function for a commodity stated in terms of his income and the prices of all commodities, it now becomes pertinent to inquire into the effects on the demand for one commodity when prices and/or income change. Since we have already observed that the demand function is homogeneous of degree zero we shall now be concerned with changes in prices and income that do not leave the quantity demanded unchanged. In order to examine, independently of each other, the effects of price and income changes, the system of equations that represent the first order conditions for the maximization of utility[5] is further differentiated. This system of equations is then solved for the

---

[5] It will be remembered that the first order conditions for a maximum are given by

$$\frac{dU}{dm} = 0 \qquad \text{or} \qquad \frac{dU}{dx} = 0.$$

unknown rates of change. After suitable manipulations a final equation can be deduced which is known as the Slutsky Equation.[6]

$$\frac{\partial x}{\partial p_x} = \left(\frac{\partial x}{\partial p_x}\right)_{U=\text{constant}} - x\left(\frac{\partial x}{\partial y}\right)_{price=\text{constant}}$$

In this equation the term on the left hand side, $\partial x/\partial p_x$, represents the rate of change of the consumer's purchases of X with respect to the changes in the price of X, p_x, while everything else is held constant. As can be seen from the Slutsky Equation, this rate of change, $\partial x/\partial p_x$, is represented as being composed of two parts. The first, or $(\partial x/\partial p_x)_{U=\text{constant}}$, stands for the change in the amount of commodity X purchased that is due to what is called the *Substitution Effect*. While the second part, or $-x(\partial x/\partial y)_{price=\text{constant}}$, represents the part of the change in the consumption of X that is due to what is called the *Income Effect*.

In order to explicate the meaning of these terms let us take the case where the price of X is observed to fall. In this case the consumer may wish to buy more of X—that is, substitute extra quantities of X for M—because (i) X has become cheaper, and/or (ii) the fall in the price of X has in effect increased the income of the consumer. The *Substitution Effect*, $(\partial x/\partial p_x)_{U=\text{constant}}$, represents the change that takes place in the consumer's purchase of X if the price change is simultaneously compensated for by a change in the consumer's income so that in effect the consumer is forced to remain on the same indifference curve as he was prior to the change in the price of X. However, since the consumer's *actual* income has been left unchanged, the *Income Effect* represents the difference between the point (the combination of X and M) given by the *Substitution Effect* and the new equilibrium point—namely, the point denoting the combination of X and M that maximizes his utility for new price of X.

To further clarify these concepts consider the following example. Take a consumer who is currently maximizing his utility subject to his budget constraint AB. Then his purchases can be represented by F, on the indifference curve U_a. (See Figure 3.)

---

[6] For the derivation of this equation see: E. E. Slutsky, "On the Theory of the Budget of the Consumer," American Economic Review, *Readings in Price Theory*, Irwin, Homewood, Illinois, 1952, pp. 27–56.

If the price of X falls, the quantity of X and M that can now be purchased is clearly greater than before. Hence, the new point of equilibrium must be on an indifference curve, say U_b, that is at a higher level of utility than U_a. We shall represent this new equilibrium point by H, lying on U_b at the point where the new budget line AC is tangent to U_b. So far, then, we have used the fall in

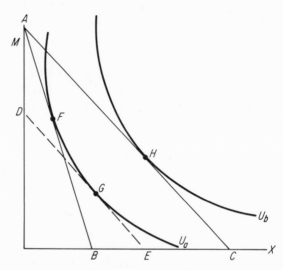

Figure 3.

price of X to show that the consumer can now purchase more of X and M, and that his increased purchases place him on a higher level of utility U_b. The Slutsky Equation refers to the movement from U_a to U_b. As we have seen, this movement from F to H can be broken down into two parts. In Figure 3 they are depicted by the changes from F to G, and from G to H. The point G is chosen because it lies on the original indifference curve U_a and because it is also the point of tangency between the curve U_a and a line DE which is drawn parallel to the new budget line AC. Since DE has the same slope as AC the ratio of the price of X to the price of M will be the same in both cases. Thus, G denotes the combination of X and M the consumer would buy if after the price of X fell his income was sufficiently reduced so that he could only obtain the same level of utility, U_a, as before. The movement from F to G corresponds to the *Substitution Effect*. In a similar manner, the movement from G to H represents the effect the fall in the price of X has on the income of the consumer, if everything else, i.e., the price of M, remains constant. This effect is called the *Income Effect*.

Having identified the effects of a price change in a consumer's purchases we shall now examine some of the further deductions that can be made about these two components. The first important inference is that the sign, or direction, of the substitution effect can be shown to always be negative. This means that if the consumer's income is continuously adjusted so that he remains on the same indifference curve, then if the price of X rises it can be concluded that the quantity of X purchased will decrease. Similarly if the price of X falls, the quantity purchased will increase. Unfortunately, the same inference cannot be made for the income effect, and $-x(\partial x/\partial y)_{price\,=\,constant}$, may be of either sign. However, if the income effect is positive and its absolute value is sufficiently large to make the entire equation positive, then the commodity X is said to be an *inferior good*. Essentially this means that as the consumer's real income rises he wishes to spend less and less of it on commodity X. Potatoes and bread are the customary examples of inferior goods. Consider for example a consumer who is sufficiently poor so that a considerable portion of his income is spent on staples like potatoes and bread. If the price of potatoes falls, or for some other reason the consumer's real income rises, then potatoes will be classified as an inferior good if the consumer with his extra income now decides to purchase fewer potatoes and more of some other more appetizing commodities.

This analysis of the effects of changes in price on the demand for one commodity can be carried a step further to account for the changes in demand for commodity A resulting from the change in the price of some other commodity B. Although somewhat less information can be deduced from the changes in demand for a commodity when there are several changes in other prices—that is, the sign of the substitution effect is now unknown—there is one notable property that can be inferred. Consider the case of n commodities and n prices. Here we shall denote by the substitution effect the change that takes place in the quantity demanded of the ith commodity as a result of a change in the price of the jth commodity. It can then be shown that the substitution effect on the ith commodity which results from a change in the jth price is the same as the substitution effect on the jth commodity that results from a change in the ith price, other things being constant. In other words, one is entitled to conclude that if a consumer's demand for Bourbon whiskey increases at the rate of "three fingers" of Bourbon per $0.50 increase in the price of a quart of Scotch, then his purchases of Scotch will also increase at the rate of "three fingers" per $0.50 increase in the price of a quart of Bourbon, all other things remaining the same.

While little further can be said about the effects on demand of changes in prices of several goods, two further conditions concerning the substitution effect still need to be mentioned. If the quantity demanded of ith commodity increases as the price of the jth is increased, then these commodities are known as *substitutes*. This condition is expressed in terms of the substitution effect notation by

$$\left(\frac{\partial x_i}{\partial p_j}\right)_{U=constant} > 0.$$

If on the other hand, $(\partial x_i/\partial p_j)_{U=constant} < 0$—that is, the quantity demanded of the ith commodity falls as the price of the jth commodity rises, then these commodities are called *complements*. Both of these effects are called *cross-substitution* effects.

2. THEORY OF REVEALED PREFERENCE

In the previous section one of the principal postulates was that the consumer possessed a utility function $U = f(x, m)$. From this postulate we were able to proceed to an examination of his indifference curves and eventually to an examination of the properties of his demand functions. A more recent approach to utility analysis, however, starts at a more fundamental level. It takes as its objective the proof of the existence and properties of the indifference map—i.e. the utility function. The goal of this approach is to show that if the observed behavior of a consumer conforms to certain postulates then both the nature and the existence of his indifference map, and hence his demand functions, can be inferred from his actions.[7]

---

[7] The theory of revealed preference was first introduced by P. A. Samuelson and is presented in some detail in *Foundations of Economic Analysis*, Harvard University Press, 1947, Chapter V.

Before we proceed to give a brief account of this approach we need to introduce some further notation. In our earlier discussion we reduced all the possible commodities that a consumer could choose from to two: X which stood for one particular commodity and M which stood for a composite commodity representing the sum total of all other commodities available to the consumer. Although the analysis could have been carried out in terms of a set of commodities $x_1, x_2, \ldots, x_n$ and their respective prices $p_1, p_2, \ldots, p_n$, the two commodities X and M were introduced for simplicity's sake. While we shall continue to discuss the theory of revealed preference in terms of X and M, it must be remembered that M stands for a long list of commodities and their respective prices. Since we wish to distinguish between the quantities of X and M purchased at different prices let p_x^0 and p_m^0 stand for a particular set of prices of X and M, and p_x^1 and p_m^1 for another set of prices. Then for the prices p_x^0 and p_m^0 the total expenditure of the consumer is $y^0 = p_x^0 x^0 + p_m^0 m^0$, where x^0 and m^0 represent the quantities of X and M purchased by the consumer at these prices. Now consider an alternative collection of commodities x^1 and m^1 that could have been purchased by the consumer at the same prices p_x^0 and p_m^0. If the consumer had purchased this second set of commodities his total expenditure would be given by $y^1 = p_x^0 x^1 + p_m^0 m^1$. Given this notation we can now go on to consider the basic postulates governing the consumer's behavior.

The first maintains that when the consumer makes his selections from the alternatives that are available to him at the time, he will prefer more to less of a given commodity, if by purchasing more of this commodity his other selections are not affected. In other words, it is postulated that the consumer will always prefer to purchase a larger than a lesser amount of M if this larger purchase of M does not affect in any way the amount of X that is available to him.

The next two postulates are concerned with interpreting the actual choices that the consumer is observed to make from the various alternative batches of commodities available to him. For example, consider two possible commodity batches: $p_x^0 x^0 + p_m^0 m^0$ and $p_x^0 x^1 + p_m^0 m^1$. We observe that when presented with a choice between these alternatives, the consumer selects $p_x^0 x^0 + p_m^0 m^0$. Then by the first postulate we can infer that $p_x^0 x^0 + p_m^0 m^0 \geqq p_x^0 x^1 + p_m^0 m^1$, or alternatively that $y^0 \geqq y^1$. That is to say, since the consumer selected y^0 in preference to y^1, and since by the first postulate y^0 costs at least as much as y^1, y^0 is said to be "revealed" to be preferred to y^1.

The second postulate states that if y^0 is revealed to be preferred to y^1, y^1 may never be revealed to be preferred to y^0. This is what is called the Two-Term Consistency Condition.[8] This postulate states that if during one period of time the consumer reveals by his purchases that y^0 is preferred to y^1, then it would be inconsistent, and hence a violation of the first postulate, if in the same situation he decided to purchase y^1 instead of y^0. If this situation arose, y^1 would be revealed preferred to y^0, and we could conclude that $y^1 \geqq y^0$. However, by his earlier selections the consumer had revealed that $y^0 \geqq y^1$. Therefore, the consumer would be declared to be inconsistent in his purchases and his behavior would not be considered to fall within the limits of this theory.

The third postulate not only requires the consumer to be consistent in his purchases but also that his revealed preferences must be transitive. For example, if y^0 is revealed to be preferred to y^1, and y^1 is revealed to be preferred to y^2, which in turn is revealed to be preferred to $y^3, \ldots$, which in turn is revealed to be preferred to y^n, y^n must never be revealed to be preferred to y^0. There must be no circularity among the revealed preferences, and the consumer must select his bundles of commodities so that his revealed preferences are transitive.

From these three postulates it can be shown that the consumer must possess an indifference map—that is, a set of indifference curves each of which represents a different level of utility, as in our earlier examples. What is more, for any particular consumer these postulates allow us to construct his indifference map by presenting him with various sets of suitably chosen commodities and prices, and simply observing his responses. It must be remembered, however, that the consumer's behavior must conform to the postulates before such experiments can be carried out.

Once the indifference curves have been ascertained we can derive all the properties of the indifference and demand curves that were

---

[8] The name for this requirement is taken from J. R. Hicks, *A Revision of Demand Theory*, Oxford University Press, New York, 1956, p. 21.

derived from the utility approach. For example, in the case where the consumer is forced to move along one indifference curve, it can be shown that the substitution effect is always negative. Also, the demand curves can be shown to be homogeneous and of degree zero. Substitutes and complements are defined in a similar manner and the equality of the cross-substitution effects can also be shown to hold true.

The chief characteristic of the Revealed Preference Theory is that continuous and differentiable functions are avoided and are replaced by expressions dealing only in finite differences. The motivation for this alteration was provided by the observation that "in the world of real phenomena all changes are necessarily finite, and instantaneous rates of change remain only limiting abstractions."[9] By reformulating the Theory of Consumer Demand in terms of expressions containing only finite differences it was felt that the theory could then be stated in terms of observable quantities and hence would be more open to verification by empirical test.

---

[9] P. A. Samuelson, *op. cit.*, p. 46.

4

The Function of Concepts
in the Theory of Demand

So far we have discussed the role of deductive schema in the analysis of scientific theories, and we have described the body of economic theory that purports to explain the behavior of consumers in the market place. Accordingly, we can now investigate the theory of demand to see whether it does in fact perform those functions that are required of it if it is to be considered a part of science.

One of the objectives of empirical science is to establish general principles by means of which the particular phenomena under consideration can be explained and predicted. These general principles are contained in the hypotheses and generalizations of which a theory is composed. In the statement of a theory, terms and concepts are used which may or may not be directly related to observational phenomena. However, if the theory is concerned with empirical phenomena, and if the theory is to meet the criterion of falsifiability, then both the theory and its concepts must refer to a particular set of empirical phenomena. While the next chapter will be concerned with examining the empirical hypotheses of the theory of demand, we shall concern ourselves in this chapter with an analysis of the empirical content of its concepts and terms.

1. THE FORMATION OF CONCEPTS IN SCIENCE[1]

At the beginning of a scientific inquiry into a new subject area the descriptions of the phenomena encountered, as well as the observed regularities and generalizations, are usually stated in terms of the vocabulary of everyday language. As the new discipline grows, new terms and concepts are introduced so that eventually a system of specialized and abstract concepts is created along with a corresponding technical vocabulary. One of the most frequent ways in which these concepts are introduced is by defining them in terms of other concepts. The term "definition," however, can be used in several different senses. In order to explore the methods by which concepts are introduced into a theory we must first examine the different ways in which a term can be defined.

---

[1] This section is particularly indebted to Carl G. Hempel's paper, "The Fundamentals of Concept Formation in Empirical Science," *International Encyclopedia of Unified Science*, University of Chicago Press, 1952, Vol. **II**, No. 7.

A. Nominal Definitions

A term or concept is introduced by what is called a *nominal definition* when the new term or expression, say A_1, is stated to be synonymous with another term or expression, say A_2, whose meaning is already understood. Thus, a definition is called nominal, if it can be put into the following form:

Let the term or expression A_1 be synonymous with the term or expression A_2. From this form we can see that a nominal definition is concerned with linguistic expressions and therefore must contain the names for these expressions. The usual way of forming a name for an expression is to put the name between single quotation marks. For example, we could characterize the definition of a 'monopolist' or an 'utility index' in the following way:

Let the term 'monopolist' be synonymous with the expression 'a market with a single seller'.

Let the term 'utility index' be synonymous with the expression 'the numbers assigned by a utility function to alternative combinations of commodities'.

The technique of identifying these expressions by means of quotation marks is not the only one that can be used. Various notations exist for denoting this relation but we shall not bother to discuss them here. The point that we wish to make is that a nominal definition can be characterized as a stipulation to the effect that the term or the expression specified by the first term, or *definiendum*, is to be considered synonymous with the term or expression specified by the second term, or *definiens*.

This method of defining a term does not have to be restricted to the case when we are introducing a new term. A nominal definition can be used to identify a term that is part of another expression, such as a property of being a monopolist. It may also be used to denote by a particular name a certain class of objects, a specific relation between objects, or a function that relates the properties of particular objects in a specified manner. Consider, for example, the definitions of the following terms taken from the theory of the firm:

An 'Isoquant' is defined to be synonymous with the expression 'the locus of all combinations of a firm's inputs that yield a specified output level'.

A 'production function' is defined to be synonymous with the expression 'the function that states the quantity of a firm's output in terms of the quantities of the variable inputs'.

The term 'marginal cost' is defined to be synonymous with the expression 'the first derivative of the total cost curve taken with respect to output'.

From these examples we can see that a nominal definition allows us to single out an expression, class, relation, or function and to replace it with a term that is frequently called a 'concept'.

It must be remembered, however, that this concept is a name and is only given a linguistic meaning by the process of stipulating that the concept shall be synonymous with another expression whose meaning is already understood.

B. Real Definitions

A "real" definition, on the other hand, is not a stipulation determining the meaning of some expression. Rather it is a definition whereby the definiens consists of a set of statements that are the necessary and sufficient conditions for the meaning of the definiendum to hold "true."[2] For example, in the theory of the firm a perfectly competitive market is asserted to exist when the following conditions are satisfied: (1) all firms produce a homogeneous product and there are no advantages or disadvantages accruing to any of these producers by selling to one customer rather than another, (2) both firms and consumers are sufficiently numerous so that the sales or purchases of each unit are small with respect to the total volume of transactions, (3) both firms and consumers have perfect knowledge of current prices and bids, and both take advantage of every opportunity to increase their respective profits or utility, and (4) there are neither costs nor restrictions on entry and exit from the market. If we label these conditions A_x, B_x, C_x, and D_x respectively, then the real definition of a competitive market, M_x, would be given by the following sentence.

X is a competitive market if and only if x satisfies the conditions A, B, C, and D. Or equivalently:

$$M_x \equiv A_x \cdot B_x \cdot C_x \cdot D_x.$$

---

[2] The meaning of this term will be discussed presently.

As can be seen from the above, the use of the equivalence sign (the 'if and only if' part) does not represent a convention concerning the use of the term M_x. Instead it is an assertion about the competitive market, M_x, which claims to be true. Since this definition constitutes an assertion that certain conditions are both necessary and sufficient for the existence of a competitive market, our next concern is to examine the ways in which such an assertion can be shown to be "true"—that is, we now wish to investigate what is meant by the word "true."

One approach to this question would be to suggest that the expression $A_x \cdot B_x \cdot C_x \cdot D_x$ is synonymous with the expression 'x is a competitive market'. In this case we have what is called an *analytic definition* of the term. In an analytic definition the meaning of the concept is given by an analysis of the meaning of the parts on the right hand side of the equivalence sign. Thus, the "truth" of the proposition

$$M_x \equiv A_x \cdot B_x \cdot C_x \cdot D_x$$

is discovered solely by an examination of the meaning of its constituent parts. No reference is made here to empirical phenomena.[3] The validation of an analytic definition is carried out by a process that is called *meaning analysis*. For example, an English dictionary provides a long list of analytic definitions, there being at least one for each word in the language. These definitions are shown to be true in the dictionary by demonstrating that, within whatever degree of approximation is allowed by the language, the meaning of the term on the left hand side of the equivalence sign is synonymous with the meaning of the terms that appear on the right hand side. In those cases where there are a number of ambiguities, several sentences are usually included to point out these differences in meaning.

Having considered the problem of validating the proposition $M_x \equiv A_x \cdot B_x \cdot C_x \cdot D_x$ when it is interpreted as an analytic definition we can now turn our attention to an alternative interpretation. Consider, for example, the case where M_x is no longer

---

[3] For an analogous method of determining the truth value of a statement the reader is referred back to the discussion on the interpretation of pure deductive systems given in Chapter 2.

considered just to have the same meaning as $A_x \cdot B_x \cdot C_x \cdot D_x$. Instead, it is now asserted that, as a matter of empirical fact, the four conditions A, B, C, and D, are simultaneously satisfied by *those and only those* phenomena which are also competitive markets. Under this interpretation the sentence $M_x \equiv A_x \cdot B_x \cdot C_x \cdot D_x$ has the characteristics of an empirical law. It can be refuted or confirmed by a direct empirical enquiry into the characteristics of competitive markets. In this case the real definition constitutes what is called an *empirical analysis* of the properties of a competitive market. Consequently, in order to test whether the definition of M_x is 'true' or 'false' we would have to conduct an empirical investigation. This investigation would be concerned with determining whether the evidence supported the following two conditions: (i) that each of the four conditions represented by A, B, C, and D can be shown to exist in market situations, and (ii) that the conditions A, B, C, D hold simultaneously in only those situations that are called competitive markets. If the empirical evidence disagrees with either of these conditions, then one can conclude that the definition is 'false' and that $M_x \equiv A_x \cdot B_x \cdot C_x \cdot D_x$ does not constitute a true definition of a competitive market.

From this discussion it should be apparent that empirical analysis, meaning analysis, and nominal definition all differ from each other. As we have just seen, empirical analysis is concerned with empirical phenomena. It states the characteristics which are, as a matter of empirical fact, both necessary and sufficient for the occurrence of the phenomena under discussion. Meaning analysis, on the other hand, deals with linguistic expressions and their meanings. Thus, an analytic definition is considered to be 'true' or 'false' depending on whether the expression on the left hand side of the equivalence sign is, or is not, synonymous with the expression on the right hand side. A nominal definition, however, is employed to introduce a new concept or term by stipulating that the new term is to be considered equivalent to some other term already a part of the vocabulary. The difference between meaning analysis and a nominal definition can be more readily perceived if one remembers that in the former the expressions on *both* sides of the equivalence sign must previously be understood, while in the latter is is only the definiens that must already be incorporated in the working vocabulary.

C. Function of Concepts in Empirical Science

In order to predict and to explain the occurrence of specific events, general relations must be established between the occurrences of different phenomena so that the occurrence of an individual event can be deduced from these general principles. Thus, one of the fundamental requirements of a science is a set of general principles and laws that permit the explanation and prediction of particular events. Clearly, to construct such laws concepts are needed that are suited to the process of constructing generalizations. In a given body of theory, then, many of the concepts will be highly abstract and will bear little direct relation to observational phenomena. If the theory is to be considered a part of empirical science certain connections must exist that link these abstract concepts to the vocabulary of observational phenomena. Unless these connections exist, the concepts and terms of the theory cannot have any empirical content, and consequently the theory as a whole cannot be considered to be a part of empirical science.

Consider, for example, a theoretical system whose terms and concepts are such that they permit the establishment of a set of general principles and laws, all of which are deducible from a set of, what we will call, basic postulates. If we represent this theory in terms of a deductive system we can immediately decide if a given conclusion or hypothesis is logically true or not—that is, if it can be legitimately inferred from the basic postulates.[4] But, to be able to test whether or not the derived conclusions are empirically true, an adequate empirical interpretation must be given to the terms and concepts embedded in the theory. Certainly not all concepts in a theory need to have direct empirical interpretations. These concepts are usually called "theoretical concepts."[5] But even though theoretical concepts have no observational counterparts, if the theoretical system of which they are a part is given

---

[4] In an analogous manner a real definition of a term is tested for its 'truth' or falsity by meaning analysis.

[5] The term "theoretical concept" is taken from R. B. Braithwaite, *op. cit.*, p. 51, and is used to identify terms like Schrüodinger's ψ function, "electric-field vector," "electron," etc., that are employed in general laws but are not themselves observational terms.

an adequate empirical interpretation, then this interpretation in turn confers empirical meaning on these constructs.

An empirical interpretation of a theory essentially plays a double role. It indirectly confers empirical content on the theoretical concepts while at the same time permitting the theory's hypotheses to be capable of refutation by empirical test. Thus, a theoretical system that lacks an adequate empirical interpretation is incapable of being tested and cannot constitute a theory of empirical phenomena.

2. CONCEPTS AND DEFINITIONS IN THE THEORY OF DEMAND

Having developed our analytic framework it is now time to proceed with the analysis. The remainder of this chapter will be devoted to an examination of both the methods used to formulate and the empirical interpretation given to the concepts and terms that are employed in the Theory of Demand. Despite the fact that this analysis will be carried out on individual concepts and terms, care will be taken not to overlook the fact that one cannot fully evaluate a concept standing by itself. That is to say, we recognize that a concept can have explanatory and predictive power only within the context of an interpreted theory.

A. The Concept of Utility

We shall start our analysis with an examination of utility theory and the concept of a utility function. In Chapter 3 we saw that a utility function is defined in terms of a consumer's purchases during a specified period of time. We also saw that if we allow X to stand for one commodity, and M to stand for a composite commodity that represents the remaining alternatives, then the utility function could be expressed as $U = f(x, m)$, where x and m represent the quantities of X and M selected.[6] Since utility functions

---

[6] It should be clear to the reader that the Hicksian utility function that we are employing can, without any alteration in the analysis, be replaced by the more general form $U_i = U_i(q_{i1}, q_{i2}, \ldots, q_{in})$, where U_i represents the utility function of the ith consumer and $q_1, q_2, \ldots, q_n$ the n commodities that he selects.

have ordinal properties, if we have two different collections of X and M—namely, (x_1, m_1) and (x_2, m_2)—then it is possible that the combination of x_1 and m_1 has a higher utility to the consumer, other things being equal, than x_2 and m_2—i.e., $U_1 > U_2$. However, before we are able to determine the truth value of such a statement we must first be sure we are clear how the concept of a "utility function" is introduced into the theory.

One possibility is that the concept of a utility function is to be considered as a real definition capable of validation by empirical analysis. In this case the statement that the ith consumer has a utility function, e.g. $U_i = f_i(x, m)$, asserts that as a matter of empirical fact consumer i has a utility function if and only if he buys a quantity of X and M, at their prevailing prices, such that $y_i = p_x x + p_m m$, where y_i represents the ith consumer's total income for the period under discussion. Since M represents all the possible commodities available to consumer i other than commodity X, the combination of $p_x x + p_m m$ *must always* represent whatever purchases consumer i makes during the specified period of time. For example, if consumer i spends 10 per cent of his income on X and all the rest on M, then this combination will satisfy the definition equally as well as a combination composed of 90 per cent of y_i spent on X and only 10 per cent spent on M. It follows, therefore, that there is no combination of X and M that will *not* satisfy the definition.[7] Yet we have already seen that if the truth value of a statement is independent of the truth values of its component parts, then it is not pertinent to submit the statement to empirical test.[8] Thus, one can conclude that the concept of a utility function cannot be considered as a real definition capable of empirical validation.

A second possibility is to consider the concept of a utility function to be introduced into the theory by an analytic definition. If this is the case, the truth or falsity of the definition can only be determined by examining the meaning of the terms contained in the two expressions. On the other hand, this concept could also

---

[7] It must be remembered that any savings or unspent monies are also considered to be contained in M.

[8] The reader is referred to the discussion on interpreting deductive systems in Chapter 2.

be interpreted as being introduced by a nominal definition where the meaning of the term 'utility function' was stipulated to be synonymous with the functional relation $f(x, m)$. In either event it is clear that, taken by itself, the truth value of the concept of a utility function cannot be determined by empirical analysis.

That this should be so is readily apparent once we consider the notion of an indifference curve. Referring again to Chapter 3 we see that an indifference curve is defined as the locus of points described by those combinations of X and M that yield for a consumer the same level of utility. Hence, the concept of an indifference curve clearly places some restrictions on the concept of a utility function. If we allow U' to represent the indifference curve that has utility U' at all points on it we can represent it by the following expression: $U' = f'(x, m)$. Now, if the concept of an indifference curve is taken to be capable of verification by empirical analysis, we can see that this would imply the following:

U'_i is an indifference curve for consumer i if and only if $U_i = U'_i$ for the combinations of X and M that satisfy $U_i = f_i(x, m)$.

This statement affirms that it is possible for consumer i to select a combination of X and M such that $U_i \neq U'_i$. However, before we can engage in an empirical analysis to find out whether this is in fact the case, we need to have some information or general principles about the behavior of consumer i. This information is provided for us by the three basic postulates of utility theory which are as follows:

P_1: For all possible pairs of alternatives A and B the consumer can state whether he prefers A to B, or B to A, or whether he is indifferent between them.[9]

P_2: For any pair of alternative A and B only one of these three possibilities may hold true at any one period of time.

P_3: If for three possible alternatives A, B, and C, the consumer prefers A to B, and B to C, then he will prefer A to C.

From these postulates we can now infer that it is quite possible for consumer i to select a combination of X and M such that $U_i \neq U'_i$. Also it is evident that if consumer i behaves in a fashion

---

[9] It should be noted that alternatives A and B each entail some combinations of X and M at their respective prices.

that is consistent with these postulates, then we can also infer that there are several combinations of X and M that will satisfy the definition of an indifference curve—that is, $U'_i = f'_i(x, m)$, where $U_i = U'_i$. Since empirical meaning has now been given to the concept of an indifference curve, the concept of a utility function is no longer devoid of empirical content. Nevertheless, it must not be forgotten that this empirical content is introduced by three postulates, P_1, P_2, and P_3. Consequently, these postulates must be subject to empirical analysis if the theory of utility is to be confirmed or disconfirmed by empirical investigations. If these postulates can be empirically verified, a question we shall examine later on, then we are now at liberty to explore the remaining important concepts in the theory of utility.

B. *Utility Maximization*

Whether one prefers the approach of the neo-classical theory of utility or that of the theory of revealed preference, the next important concept that we shall examine is the concept of a maximum of utility. Now a utility function is defined in terms of combinations of commodities. Therefore, the point at which a consumer reaches a maximum of utility must be defined in terms of a particular set of commodities.

From the analysis presented in Chapter 3 we know that both the first order and second order conditions must be satisfied if this maximum is to exist. The first order condition ensures that we have reached a point where there is either a maximum, minimum, or a saddle point. The second order condition tells us which one of these possibilities is in fact the case. From these conditions it is possible, both in the theory of utility and the theory of revealed preference, to infer that the indifference curves can be represented by a family of rectangular hyperbolas. We can also infer that the ith consumer's utility is at a maximum at the point at which his budget equation is tangent to one of his indifference curves. (See pp. 34–37). This maximum can also be demonstrated to be unique. Hence, it will be sufficient for our purposes to restrict our attention to the first order conditions.

Since there is only one point at which a maximum can occur,

this point, or combination of commodities, can be represented by the following:

U^* is a point of maximum utility if and only if the quantities selected of X and M are such that $dU/dm = 0$—that is, the point at which the budget equation $y = p_x x + p_m m$ is tangent to the indifference curve $U^* = f^*(x, m)$.

For this concept to be substantiated by empirical analysis we must be able to test whether a particular selection of commodities provides a maximum of utility for consumer i or not. Our earlier analysis showed that the first order condition was met when the ratio of the prices of X and M was equal to the ratio of the marginal utility of X to the marginal utility of M for consumer i.[10] Since the utility function has only ordinal properties, the concept of marginal utility, denoted in equation (3.6) by f_1 or f_2, has no empirical interpretation. Previously, we pointed out that the ratio of the price of X to the price of M was also equal to the slope of the indifference curve.[11] It follows, therefore, that the empirical criterion of whether a specified set of commodities yields a maximum of utility for consumer i can now be stated in terms of the ratio of the prices of X and M and the slope of his indifference curve. If both of these ratios are empirically determinable, then it will be possible to test whether a given set of commodities does in fact yield a maximum of utility for consumer i.

Unfortunately, it is not immediately clear whether these ratios are in fact empirically determinable. To know the ratio of p_x to p_m, for example, implies that we know the price of commodity X as well as the price of the composite commodity M. Now the price of X is easily obtained from direct observation. But what about the price of M? After all, M represents all the remaining commodities available to consumer i during the specified interval of time, and m that subset of M that was selected at price p_m. Hence, the exact empirical meaning of this price ratio is not at all clear. Consider also what is meant by the slope of the indifference curve. Analytically, it means the rate at which consumer i would

---

[10] See equation (3.6), p. 34.
[11] See equation (3.3), p. 32.

be willing to substitute X for M and M for X. But how is this slope to be interpreted empirically?

The normal procedure in economic analysis for handling both of these problems is to take the case of a restricted number of actual commodities, preferably two, and treat all the remaining commodities and prices as fixed. The selected commodities are then examined, one at a time, to determine the price ratios and a linear approximation to the slope of the indifference surface. Such a procedure, however, does not provide us with a very satisfactory empirical interpretation. At best it relies on the economist's ability to identify each of the relevant commodities as substitutes or complements of each other (concepts that will be examined below). Further, this comparison of the price ratios and the slope of the indifference curve has empirical meaning if and only if a fourth postulate about the consumer's behavior is empirically true.

P_4: The consumer will purchase that combination of commodities that yields him the highest level of utility.

If this postulate is supported by the relevant empirical tests,[12] then, however difficult in practice, it would at least in principle be possible to empirically ascertain whether or not the price ratios were equal to the slope of the indifference curve. We can conclude, therefore, that the empirical validity of the concept of a maximum of utility also depends on the ability to confirm the basic postulates, P_1, P_2, P_3, and P_4 by empirical tests.

C. Substitutes and Complements

As noted above, the empirical interpretation of whether a consumer has maximized his utility or not rests in part upon the identification of the commodities that he selects as substitutes or complements. In the previous chapter, it will be remembered, the concepts 'substitute' and 'complement' were defined in terms of the effects on the demand for the ith commodity when the price of the jth commodity was altered, while the utility derived from the purchase and all other prices were kept constant. These concepts were expressed more formally by the following notation:

---

[12] We shall examine this question at length later on.

Commodity x_i is a substitute if and only if

$$\left(\frac{\partial x_i}{\partial p_j}\right)_{U=constant} > 0$$

Commodity x_i is a complement if and only if

$$\left(\frac{\partial x_i}{\partial p_j}\right)_{U=constant} < 0$$

From these definitions it is evident that if we wish to be able to establish whether or not a given commodity is a substitute for consumer i, we must first find a situation in which the prices of all commodities except x_j remain unchanged. Once this situation has been discovered we must then observe the effects of the change in the price of x_j, on his purchases of x_i. Further, since the utility derived from this new selection of commodities must remain constant, not only must consumer i be indifferent between these two alternatives, but we also must have some method for determining whether the utility derived from the new purchases has been held constant or not. Consequently, to be able to ascertain whether commodity x_i is a substitute or not, we need to be able to submit the ith consumer's utility function to empirical analysis.

We have already seen, however, that the concept of a utility function derives its empirical content from the concept of an indifference curve. In turn, the indifference curve is given empirical meaning if and only if the behavior of consumer i conforms to the postulates P_1, P_2, and P_3. We have also seen that the notion of a maximum of utility depends in part on the economist's ability to identify whether a given set of commodities are substitutes or complements. Therefore, it follows that the source of empirical content for all these concepts lies in the four basic postulates of behavior. If these postulates can be empirically confirmed, then these concepts can be subjected to empirical analysis. And the implications of this theory can then be tested by confrontation with observed behavior.

D. The Demand Curve

The last important concept we shall examine in detail is that of the demand curve itself. As noted in Chapter 3, demand curves for particular commodities can be directly derived from the first order conditions of utility maximization. These curves are single valued functions and are stated in terms of prices and income. The dependent variable is the commodity that is currently under consideration. This means that the demand function for commodity X for the ith consumer can be expressed as before by:

$$x_i = \frac{y_i}{2p_{x_i}} \tag{4.1}$$

or in more general terms by

$$D_{ij}(x_j) = f_{ij}(p_1 \, p_2 \ldots p_m, y_i) \tag{4.2}$$

where $$p_1, p_2, \ldots, p_m$$

represent the prices of all the relevant commodities, and D_{ij} represents the ith consumer's demand function for the jth commodity x_j. As in the previous cases it is easy to show that this definition of a demand curve, if considered in terms of a real definition, is analytically true. That is to say, the meaning of the expression on the left hand side is in agreement with the meaning customarily given to the expression on the right hand side. What we are interested in examining, however, is whether the components of this definition have sufficient empirical interpretations so that the definition, by itself, is open to empirical analysis.

Taking the first definition (4.1) we have the ith consumer's demand for X stated in terms of his income and the prevailing price p_x. Manifestly, if this is all there really were to the demand for X, then there would be no questioning the empirical content of this function. For in this case all we would have to know is the ith consumer's income, and the prevailing price of X, in order to predict forthwith the quantity that he would consume. Unfortunately, the situation is not quite so simple as it might seem. The first point to note is that the demand functions themselves are derived from the theory of utility under the condition that consumer i *is* maximizing his utility, and we have already examined the problems involved in trying to determine when consumer i is maximizing his utility. If, therefore, the empirical validity of the demand function is to rest solely on the condition that the consumer is at all times maximizing his utility, then we are back to the position where the empirical content of these concepts rests entirely upon the empirical validity of the four basic postulates.

Our current concern then is to examine these demand functions to see whether there is some further basis for empirical interpretation such that the empirical content of the entire theory need not be contingent upon the four postulates.

To start with, if we take the case where we are dealing with the two commodities X and M, the ith consumer's demand for X will be a single valued function of the price of X and his income. However, this function is derived by taking partial differentials with respect to X—that is, by holding the price and quantity of M constant. Therefore, this demand function can only represent the ith consumer's demand for X in the case where everything except the price of X is held constant.

In the case of the more generalized demand function, we have the ith consumer's demand for commodity x_j expressed as a function of the prices of all other commodities as well as of the consumer's income. Yet in this case the form of the function is not defined in any detail. For example, if we wished to investigate the effects of changes in the prices of some commodities on the demand for x_j we would have to employ the analytic framework given to us by the Slutsky Equation. In other words, to be able to examine the effects of price changes on the demand for x_j, we would need to identify and compute the substitution and income effects. To determine the substitution effect we need to vary the price of x_j while, by suitable manipulations of his income, the consumer is kept on the same indifference curve. However, before we can subject the concept of a substitution effect to empirical analysis we need to have some technique for finding out whether the ith consumer has been kept on the same indifference curve throughout the operation. An examination of the income effect is no less difficult since in this case we are concerned with keeping *all* prices constant while income is allowed to vary. The algebraic sum of these two effects gives us the rate at which the ith consumer changes his purchases of x_j with respect to the changes in the price of x_j, while all other prices and income are held constant. Hence, although we started with a generalized demand function, the only way in which the concepts and components of the function can be analyzed is by treating the world as though one thing varied while everything else remained constant. In fact we have not improved on our earlier position. At that point there were only two commodities and the empirical content of these functions depended upon the empirical truth value of the postulates.

There is one further property of demand curves that still remains to be examined. It is the condition that the slope of the demand curve for x_j is almost always negative. We have just noted that the rate of change of the quantity demanded of x_j with respect to the price of x_j can be broken down into substitution and income effect components. Since the slope of the demand curve is expressed by this rate of change we can see that the sum of the substitution and income effects should also be a negative number. However, demand curves are not *always* negatively sloped—that is, the demand for some commodities increases as the price rises. Perfumes, items of jewelry, and fur capes are examples of some articles that frequently have positively sloped demand curves. Therefore, the negative slope cannot, without further qualifications, be taken as a universal, empirical property of these curves. For example, it will be remembered from our earlier discussion that the slope of the demand curve, i.e. $\partial x_i / \partial p_j$, is negative if and only if the absolute value of the income effect, i.e.

$$\left| -x_i \left(\frac{\partial x_i}{\partial y} \right)_{price=constant} \right|$$

is not sufficiently large to make $\partial x_i / \partial p_j$ also positive in value. That is to say, it is only the substitution effect, i.e.

$$\left(\frac{\partial x_i}{\partial p_j} \right)_{U=constant}$$

which always has a negative value. If the absolute value of the income effect is greater than the absolute value of the substitution effect, then the demand curve will have a positive slope. Now the empirical confirmation of the basic postulates has already been shown to be a prerequisite for the actual determination of the substitution and income effects. Therefore, without further qualifications, the property of a negative slope does not provide any direct, additional empirical interpretation.

CONCLUSIONS

From this analysis it has become apparent that the concepts of the economic theory of consumer behavior are open to empirical analysis if and only if the four postulates of the theory of utility are themselves confirmable by empirical investigations. This is not to say that there are no other ways of introducing empirical content into these concepts. It is rather that our investigation has shown that unless these postulates are empirically confirmed then the remaining sources of empirical interpretation cannot be employed. This is an important conclusion. It asserts that these concepts must be classified as theoretical concepts until it is demonstrated that the postulates of the theory of utility are supported, and not disconfirmed, by empirical tests.

Since the theory of demand can only apply to those consumers whose behavior accords with these basic postulates we shall now turn our attention to an examination of the conditions under which these postulates can be empirically confirmed. If these postulates are to be considered a part of a theoretical structure whose function is to explain and predict consumer behavior, then we must also examine the function of postulates and laws in the explanation and prediction of particular events. It is toward both of these tasks that the next two chapters are devoted.

5

The Function of Laws
in the Theory of Demand

In the previous chapter we examined in some detail the concepts and terms employed in the theory of consumer behavior as well as their possible sources of empirical interpretation. Since concepts and terms are introduced into a theoretical system in order to formulate general laws and hypotheses, it is only within the context of such a theoretical system that a concept can have explanatory and predictive power. Accordingly, our intention is to examine the function of these laws, and thus of the concepts as well, in the "explanation" and "prediction" of economic events.[1] In so doing we shall make a point of investigating the ways in which the postulates about consumer behavior can be subjected to a process of refutation by empirical test.

1. THE FUNCTION OF GENERAL LAWS IN EXPLANATION AND PREDICTION[2]

A. General Laws

In the literature of the physical sciences the term "general law" is usually taken to mean a universal statement of conditional form,[3] stated in such a manner that it can be subjected to confirmation or disconfirmation by empirical test. A statement is

---

[1] While a large number of books and articles have been written on the subject of "explanation" and "prediction," both in the social as well as in the physical sciences, with which the author has no desire to compete, there are a sufficient number of differences in these explications to leave in doubt precisely what is meant by these terms. Because the analysis in this essay involves the explicit use of these terms, our presentation will be greatly facilitated if both reader and author can agree, for the purposes of this essay, on one meaning for these terms.

[2] This section is indebted to the excellent paper by Carl G. Hempel, "The Function of General Laws in History," *Journal of Philosophy*, Vol. 39, 1942, pp. 35–48. (Reprinted in H. Feigl and W. Sellars, *Readings in Philosophical Analysis*, New York, 1949.)

[3] The term "conditional" refers to the form in which the statement is expressed. We have represented the conditional in our logical notation by '$\rightarrow$' (see Chapter 2). Hence, the statement "all P's are Q's" is of universal and conditional form if we construe it as stating for all values (x_i) of x it is the case that $Px_i \rightarrow Qx_i$.

universal if it asserts that *every* occurrence of a specific kind of event is *always* related in a particular manner to the occurrence of another specified kind of event.

For example, the well-known law relating the free fall of a body near the earth's surface to its acceleration is given by $d^2s/dt^2 = 32$. That this is a universal statement is attested by the fact that the equation asserts that *every* body which is near the earth and is freely falling will fall with an acceleration of 32 feet per second per second. That this statement is classified as a general law is attested by the fact that it is stated in such a manner that it can be subjected to a process of refutation by empirical test. If the law had been stated as $d^2s/dt^2 = 17.5$, it would not have been long before counter examples were discovered and the universal applicability of the law challenged.

It should be noted that while a universal statement is not considered to be a general law unless it can be subjected to empirical test, it does not follow that all general laws are in fact well confirmed by empirical evidence. The criteria that allow one to determine whether a law is satisfactorily confirmed are distinct from those that allow one to determine whether it is possible to subject a general statement to an empirical test. We are concerned with the function of laws in a theoretical system and the criteria by which they can be adjudged to be refutable by empirical test. Thus, the problems associated with determining the "degree of confirmation" will not be further considered.[4]

For our purposes a general law will be taken to assert the following type of regularity: for *every* occurrence of a particular kind of event O during a definite spatio-temporal interval a specific kind of event E will occur at a place and time that is related in a specified manner to the place and time of the occurrence of the event O.[5]

---

[4] For an analysis of the problems involved in determining whether a law is satisfactorily confirmed or not see: Rudolf Carnap, "Remarks on Induction and Truth", *Philosophy and Phenomenological Research*, Vol. 6, 1946, pp. 590–602; and Karl R. Popper, *op. cit.*, Ch. 10.

[5] The reader will note that we have made no attempt to include statements containing probabilistic elements in our definition of a general law. This is not because they are not interesting or useful formulations, but because we have elected to treat the special problems incurred with the use of probabilistic hypotheses at a later point in this essay.

B. Explanation

Since general laws relate, in a specified manner, the occurrence of one specific kind of event to another, they are used to connect specific events into particular patterns that are referred to as "explanations." When explaining the occurrence of a particular kind of event E, the customary procedure is to point to a list of factors $O_1\tau_1, O_2\tau_2, \ldots, O_n\tau_n$ that are said to have determined the occurrence of $E_n\tau$. By asserting that this particular set of events $O_1\tau_1, O_2\tau_2, \ldots, O_n\tau_n$ caused (or determined) the particular event $E\tau$ we are actually asserting that there is at least one general law that relates events of kind O_i to events of kind E in a known and testable manner.[6] By restating this in a more rigorous manner we can see that the "scientific explanation"[7] of the occurrence of the event E consists in:

(1) A set of statements that assert the occurrence of specific events
$$O_1\tau_1, O_2\tau_2, \ldots, O_n\tau_n.$$

(2) A general law or set of general laws stated in such a fashion that:

(i) both the general laws and the statements concerning the events $O_1\tau_1, O_2\tau_2, \ldots, O_n\tau_n$ are subject to confirmation by empirical test,

(ii) both the general laws and the statements $O_1\tau_1, O_2\tau_2, \ldots, O_n\tau_n$ are satisfactorily confirmed by empirical evidence,

(iii) the occurrence of the event $E\tau$ can be logically deduced from the conjunction of the general laws and the statements asserting the occurrence of the events $O_1\tau_1, O_2\tau_2, \ldots, O_n\tau_n$.

---

[6] Throughout the following discussion the set of events $O_1, O_2, \ldots, O_n$ and E are assumed to have occurred at particular places and time periods. Hence the notation $O_1\tau_1, O_2\tau_2, \ldots, O_n\tau_n$ and $E\tau$ is used where τ refers to the place and time during which the events O_i and E occurred. The symbols $O_1, O_2, \ldots, O_n$ and E refer to the *kinds of* or *properties of* the events under consideration.

[7] The term "scientific explanation" has no honorific connotations. It is employed to distinguish the type of explanation presented in this essay from teleological, and other types of explanations found in scientific literature. In the remainder of this paper the terms "scientific explanation" and "explanation" will be used interchangeably.

For an explanation of a particular event in the physical sciences the statements in (1) would correspond to the statements specifying the initial and boundary conditions from which with the aid of the general laws contained in (2) the final event $E\,\tau$ can be deduced. To further clarify what is meant by an explanation of an event consider the following illustration:

The event that we wish to explain consists in the cracking of a container of water when it is left in a refrigerated enclosure overnight. In this case, the statements described in (1) may be given by these observations: a container with a securely fitting top is filled with distilled water. The container is then placed within a special enclosure and left there overnight. The temperature inside the enclosure is kept at 15°F and the air pressure is observed to be normal. The pressure required to burst the material of the water container is a certain number of pounds per square inch. Now the statements in (2) would be "empirical laws"[8] of the following sort: A quantitative law relating the change of the pressure of water to its temperature and volume. A law stating the temperature at which distilled water freezes given normal atmospheric pressure. And a law stating how the pressure of a mass of water behaves when the volume is not allowed to increase and the temperature is lowered sufficiently to allow the water to freeze.

From the initial and boundary conditions and the empirical laws the cracking of the water container during the night can be logically deduced. All the requirements for an explanation of the event have been fulfilled; and it can be said that a scientific explanation of the cracking of the water container has been established.

While this illustration may appear quite obvious to some readers there are several important points that should be noted:

(i) The system consisting of the water container and the refrigerated enclosure can be considered, for the purposes of this explanation, to be a closed system. Ideally the list of relevant initial and boundary conditions can be stated exhaustively.

---

[8] The term "empirical law" is used to identify general laws that are considered to be satisfactorily confirmed by empirical evidence.

(ii) The laws are universal and conditional statements that can be subjected to empirical confirmation independently from their use in the particular explanation given above.

(iii) The statements containing the initial and boundary conditions describe the occurrence of events of certain kinds $(O_1, O_2, \ldots, O_n, E)$ at certain particular spatio-temporal locations $(tau_1, tau_2, \ldots, tau_n, tau)$.

Point (iii) is particularly important. There is a significant difference between trying to establish an explanation for an event that is described by reference to its properties and its spatio-temporal position rather than for an event that is described solely in terms of the time and place in which it occurred. In the former case the explanation of the event is established, as we have seen, by deducing the occurrence of the event in question from the conjunction of the initial and boundary conditions and the relevant general laws. In the latter case, however, we are confronted with the problem of trying to establish an explanation for a particular event that is described solely by reference to the time and place in which it occurred. To develop an explanation for such an event the statement of initial and boundary conditions would have to include all the properties of the object involved as well as those of the spatial region that it occupied for the duration of the event under consideration. The impossibility of such a task is readily apparent if we consider the problem of trying to establish explanations for events such as: a particular fall in the prices of certain securities on the stock market, fluctuations in the price of gold in London during a particular time interval, the collection of commodities that are sold by a department store during a particular shopping day, or any one of an indefinitely large number of individual events. This is not to say that a description of what occurred at a particular time and place cannot be made more inclusive and detailed, but rather that it is not possible to establish a scientific explanation for an event that is described solely in terms of its spatio-temporal location.

From this discussion it is apparent that it is possible to determine whether any given explanation is a scientific explanation or not. It is evident that one of the principal criteria is that the laws or hypotheses[9] employed in the explanation be both of universal form and empirically testable. Another is that at least one of these laws must be an empirical law–that is, a law well confirmed by empirical evidence–and further that the initial and boundary conditions must be stated in observational terms.

The testability requirement does not imply that each hypothesis in the theoretical structure be directly and independently refutable by empirical test. To insist on this criterion would imply, as we have seen, that all general laws containing theoretical concepts would have to be rejected. Such a position would seriously undermine a number of theoretical structures. Under this rule we would automatically have to reject such concepts as Schrüodinger's ψ function in wave mechanics, as well as all the concepts of the theory of demand examined in the last chapter. Clearly this is not an acceptable procedure. The problem is resolved by allowing (as in the case of the empirical analysis of concepts) the testability of the hypothesis containing theoretical concepts to be determined by the testability of the empirical hypotheses that are deducible from them. If these procedures are followed the testability of the theoretical hypotheses is ensured and they may be employed in the establishment of scientific explanations.[10]

C. Prediction

The term prediction is usually employed to denote statements which assert the occurrence of an event, or set of events. The assertion of the occurrence of an event, say $E\tau$, is usually arrived at by deducing $E\tau$ from the statement of some initial and boundary conditions $(O_1\tau_1, O_2\tau_2, \ldots, O_n\tau_n)$ and the appropriate general laws. Thus, the logical structure of a scientific prediction is similar to that of a scientific explanation, and the function of the general

---

[9] In the remainder of the discussion the term "hypothesis" will be used as an equivalent of the term "general law". Hence, the term "empirical hypothesis" will be taken to be equivalent to the term "empirical law".

[10] The term "testability" is employed to denote the ability of the hypothesis or theory to stand up to—that is, not to be disconfirmed by—a series of empirical tests.

laws is the same in both cases.[11] The two are distinguished by the fact that in prediction we infer a statement about the occurrence of an event $E\tau$ before we examine whether it has occurred or not, while in an explanation it is the known occurrence of the event $E\tau$ that we wish to explain.

In science the prediction of an event is frequently used as an empirical test of one or more of the general laws in a theoretical structure. If the predicted event fails to occur, under the specified conditions, then at least one of the general laws is said to be disconfirmed. If the event does occur the law or laws are said to have passed an empirical test and their "degree of confirmation"[12] is raised.

It should be noted that the strict disconfirmation of a law or laws can only occur under the following conditions:

(i) At least one of the laws in the relevant theoretical structure is empirically well confirmed.

(ii) The system under investigation can be considered, for the purposes of the predictive inference and the subsequent

---

[11] To emphasize the logical similarity between explanation and prediction Reichenbach called them "postdictability" and "predictability": see Hans Reichenbach, *Philosophical Foundations of Quantum Mechanics*, University of California Press, 1944, p. 13. It should be noted that these points will be further discussed when we examine probabilistic explanations and predictions in the next chapter.

[12] While a discussion of the various procedures for determining the degree of confirmation goes beyond the scope of our analysis, the following quotation may serve to illustrate the meaning of the term.

> *We cannot verify the law, but we can test it by testing its single instances i.e. the particular sentences which we derive from the law and from other sentences established previously. If in the continued series of such testing experiments no negative instance is found, but the number of positive instances increases then our confidence in the law will grow step by step. Thus, instead of verification, we may speak here of gradually increasing* confirmation *of the law.*
> (R. Carnap, "Testability and Meaning," *Philosophy of Science*, Vol. 3, No. 4, 1936, p. 425).

The term "degree of confirmation" is defined and discussed in Carl G. Hempel and P. Oppenheim, "A Definition of 'Degree of Confirmation'," *Philosophy of Science*, Vol. 12, No. 2, 1945, pp. 98–115.

analysis, to be free from any significant external disturbances.

If under these conditions the predicted event does not occur then we can conclude that at least one of the general laws contained in the theory has been disconfirmed. In cases where it is either very difficult or impossible to tell whether significant disturbances have occurred or not, it is no longer possible to strictly disconfirm a law. Nevertheless, unless the first condition is met it is not possible to disconfirm *any* of the laws and hence the theoretical system cannot be considered to be a part of empirical science.[13]

2. EXPLANATION AND PREDICTION IN THE THEORY OF DEMAND

In the preceding section we have outlined and deliberately emphasized the basic requirements for a scientific explanation. We now intend to examine the theory of demand to see whether the explanations of economic events offered by this theory conform to these requirements.

A. Testing the Postulates of Utility Theory

Before we examine the explanations of economic events offered by the theory of demand we must first be sure that the theory itself is open to empirical investigation—that is, we need to make sure that there is at least one law or hypothesis within the theoretical structure that is empirically well confirmed.

In the previous chapter we saw that if the concepts of the theory were to be subjected to empirical analysis then the four basic postulates must be shown to be empirically true. If these postulates can be evinced to be well confirmed, then they will perform for us two vital functions. First they will provide the concepts of the theory with the desired empirical content. Second, having been confirmed by empirical tests, they would in turn become the empirical laws that are required to form the basis for the theory's testability. Thus, if these postulates can be demon-

---

[13] This point will be discussed at greater length in Chapter 6.

strated to be empirically true the concepts as well as the theory become testable and, in principle, meet the requirement that they are subject to the process of refutation by empirical test.

If the basic postulates of utility theory are to be accepted as empirical laws, then, as we have seen, it must be possible to state them in the universal and conditional form. Under these conditions the four basic postulates noted in Chapter 3 are now to be tested as conditional statements that apply to the behavior of all consumers. In order to see what this requirement entails let us re-examine for a moment these four postulates stated explicitly in the conditional form.

P_1: If the consumer is confronted with all possible pairs of alternatives A and B, then he can state whether he prefers A to B, or B to A, or whether he is indifferent between them.[14]

P_2: If the consumer is confronted with a pair of alternatives A and B, then he can state unequivocally whether he prefers A to B, B to A, or whether he is indifferent between them.

P_3: If the consumer is confronted with three possible alternatives A, B, and C, and the consumer states that he prefers A to B and B to C, then he will prefer A to C.

P_4: If the consumer is required to select a combination of commodities from those that are available to him, then he will select that combination that yields him the highest utility.[15]

Having stated the postulates in this form it is now necessary to decide upon the type of evidence that will be considered to provide an adequate set of empirical tests. In other words are we

---

[14] It should be noted that alternatives A and B each entail some combination of commodities at their respective prices. In order to include the notion of choice among uncertain prospects, A and B can be taken to represent certain combinations of lottery tickets. In this case the consumer's behavior must conform to slightly different postulates; but most of the essential requirements are contained in the postulates treated above, and the special conditions of the Von Neumann-Morgenstern postulates will not be treated here.

[15] In the case where uncertain prospects are involved this postulate is satisfied if the consumer is shown to maximize the expected value of his utility.

to interpret these postulates as referring directly to the behavior of individual consumers, a statistically "average" consumer, or only to an "ideal" consumer who is not expected to have any precise counterpart in "real" life?

If we adopt the last position–that is, consider only the behavior of an "ideal" consumer to be regulated by these four postulates— then we need to have a set of instructions or interpretative rules that tell us how to apply the "ideal" laws to the data of a particular case. For example, earlier in this chapter we made use of the physical law relating the free fall of a body near the earth's surface as an illustration of what was meant by a universal statement in conditional form. Now this law was formulated to be, and in fact is, an idealization of the behavior of freely falling bodies near the the earth's surface. This "ideal" law is supposed to be true only for bodies falling *in vacuo* when near the earth's surface. Since it is not possible to measure the free fall of bodies in a perfect vacuum various interpretive rules must be set out so that the law can be tested by observing free fall of bodies in the atmosphere. In this case the interpretive rules consist of a set of instructions that identify the factors to take into consideration, e.g., the density of the media, the shape of the object, etc., as well as the effect that these factors will have on the results.[16]

If we consider our postulates in this manner, e.g., as "ideal" laws, we still need to decide whether the data we wish to test the postulates against should be generated by individual consumers or by a statistically "average" consumer. Since the postulates as stated above can be construed to refer to the behavior of individual consumers, let us first consider the problem of testing these "ideal" laws against the behavior of particular consumers.[17] In order to

---

[16] It should be noted that the natural sciences frequently use this technique for formulating laws which hold true only in "ideal" cases. Almost all the well known physical laws are formulated under such conditions. Thus, as long as a set of interpretive rules exists these laws can be tested against actual instances and the data employed to confirm or disconfirm the general laws.

[17] The author is aware of the fact that many economists agree with Hicks when he states that, "To assume that the representative consumer acts like an ideal consumer is a hypothesis worth testing; to assume that an actual person, the Mr. Brown or Mr. Jones who lives around the corner, does in fact act in such a way does not deserve a moment's consideration." *A Revision of Demand Theory,*

perform these tests, what are our interpretive rules going to be? Neither utility theory nor the theory of demand provide us with much in the way of interpretive rules. The Von Neumann-Morgenstern approach enables us, under very special circumstances, to calculate the utility a particular consumer ascribes to a given selection of lottery tickets, but what about the consumer who is faced by the more common task of selecting his purchases from a wide range of commodities? For example, if we are to be able to test the "ideal" laws against the behavior of a consumer, we must have some means of determining that the consumer's preference orderings remain the same throughout the series of trials in which we observe his choice behavior. However, the theory does not provide us with a means for determining the preference orderings before the experiments begin. On the contrary, the theory only allows us to glean information about his preferences *after* he has made his selections. This fact is amply demonstrated by the approach used in the Theory of Revealed Preferences. Unless we have some independent information on the way in which a consumer's tastes alter over time we are unable to conclude very much from the data that would be generated from a series of empirical tests. It could be argued that we should assume that preferences remain the same over brief intervals of time, and conduct the test within these intervals of time, but this would not solve the problem at all. We would still have to be able to demonstrate by some alternative technique that his preferences did in fact remain unchanged during these intervals of time. For example, the problem can be stated in the following way:

If preferences are constant, then we can use the data from various trials to test the "ideal" laws. Restating this in our simplified logical notation, we have $P_t \rightarrow D_t$, where P_t represents a statement about the constancy of a consumer's preferences during a specified interval of time, and D_t a statement about the data that are generated from the empirical tests.

From our discussion in Chapter 2 it is evident that even if the

---

op. cit., p. 55. But, since few reasons are ever given why this should be so, and since the theory of demand is frequently alleged to pertain to individual consumer behavior, a consideration of the problems involved in testing the "ideal" laws against individual behavior should not be left out of our analysis.

empirical data confirm the statement D_t, we cannot employ this result to infer the empirical truth value of P_t. This is a very important point. It implies that it is not possible to use the data from one set of trials to confirm the truth values of both the major and minor premiss of a particular expression. If we had an independent method of testing the truth value of P_t, then we could employ the data from a set of trials to confirm or disconfirm the expression $P_t \rightarrow D_t$. However, an independent test for P_t is not provided by utility theory or the theory of demand. Consequently, we can conclude that to be able to test the "ideal" laws against individual behavior we first need to have an independent means of determining a consumer's preferences as well as the way in which they alter over time.

Since the interpretive rules are not sufficient to allow us to confront the "ideal" laws with individual behavior, we shall now examine whether they are sufficient to allow us to confront the "ideal" laws with "statistically" average behavior. In this case there is an abundance of data to draw on. Representative, or statistically average, patterns of behavior can be collected by gathering data on the behavior of a large number of different groups, purchasing the same or different commodities. However, it does not appear that this abundance of data facilitates the testing procedure in any way.

Consider the following example: Data are collected on the purchases of a particular commodity by the consumers of a specific region, and we now want to use these data to test our "ideal" laws. Presumably, the one law that we would like to establish is that these consumers are consistent in their choices and show no tendencies toward violation of the transitivity requirement. Yet, before our data could tell us anything about the transitivity of their selections, we would first need to know something about their preference scales. If this group of consumers is composed of individuals who are identical in every way (by this we mean that they must have identical tastes, as well as incomes) then each consumer's preference scale is exactly the same, and the group's preferences are given by aggregating the preferences of all the individuals. Except for scale factors, the group's indifference curves would be identical to each individual's. Under these conditions the data on the group's purchases could then be viewed as representing each individual's purchases and we would be ready to begin our tests. But, if we use these data to establish the preference scales, which clearly must be done prior to examining whether the preference orderings are consistent or not, we are manifestly in the same predicament as we were in our previous example.

Unless preference orderings can be established prior to and independently of the collection of the data, it is meaningless to examine the data with the hope of both establishing the preference orderings and of using these orderings for an empirical test of the "ideal" laws. For example, assume for the moment that we have been able to collect data on the purchases of a particular group of consumers. These consumers have identical tastes and incomes so that the indifference curves for the group differ only by a scale factor from the indifference curves of each member of the group. Also, assume that our data reflect only the purchases of comestibles made by this group during a particular period of time. Accordingly, the data will consist of an itemized list of foodstuffs giving the amount purchased of each at its prevailing price. Now, we can use these data to establish some kind of preference scale for these consumers for their particular selection of edibles. We can observe which items were selected and which were ignored from the list of available commodities. What we cannot do, however, is use the same collection of data to declare that the preference scale is consistent, that all alternatives were rank ordered prior to the selection taking place, and that the group chose that set of comestibles that yielded them the highest utility.

To be able to employ these data to draw this set of conclusions, we would need to have some independent method of establishing the group's preference ordering for *all* the available commodities prior to their selection of a particular set of goods. That is to say, we would need to know, before they made their selections, precisely which items should be selected and which should be avoided if their selections are to be consistent with their preference scale. Unfortunately, the only available data are the data generated by their actual selections, and these data are simply not sufficient to both determine and adjudge the preference orderings.

To further illustrate this point let us take the case of the binary choice experiment, since it has frequently been used in empirical investigations of utility theory. In this experiment the subject is required to choose one of two possible symbols in each of a fairly long series of trials. When he has selected a symbol, say a plus or a minus sign, he is told whether he was "right" or "wrong". "Correct" choices are determined by the experimenter, and these may conform to a random series of digits or they may fit a definite pattern. In either event, suppose that the "pluses" appear three-quarters of the time, determined at random while the "minuses" appear on the remaining one-quarter of the trials. If we are testing the subject to see whether his behavior conforms to the Von Neumann-Morgenstern postulates, we will want to know whether the subject maximizes his expected utility or not. In this example a subject maximizes his expected utility by choosing "plus" on every single trial. By this technique he would be correct three-quarters of the time which is a better score than he could expect to achieve by any other strategy. Hence, by observing a subject's behavior we can immediately tell whether he is or is not maximizing his expected utility and consequently whether his behavior conforms to the basic postulates of behavior or not.

What is there about this experiment that differs from our previous examples? For in the binary choice experiment it appears that we can indeed tell from the evidence of the experiment whether in fact the subject's behavior conforms to the basic postulates or not. The difference lies in the simple fact that in the case of the binary choice experiment we know precisely what behavior patterns will conform to the basic postulates. Furthermore, we have this knowledge *prior to* and *independently of* the evidence from any particular experiment. In our earlier examples we do not have this knowledge, and we cannot tell beforehand exactly what behavior will conform with and what behavior will conflict with our "ideal" laws. As a result, the evidence from any particular set of observations of consumer behavior can only tell us something about their preference structure. Unless we already know what it means in that particular situation to maximize utility (whether expected utility or not), the data cannot be used to disconfirm the postulates or laws of behavior. If the theory of demand contained interpretive rules that prescribed various sets of behavior to be consistent, in certain situations, with its "ideal" laws, then one could proceed to observe the behavior of individuals and groups and conclude from these observations whether the laws were confirmed or not. However, until such interpretive rules are specified, it is simply not possible to observe the purchases made by particluar groups of consumers and use these data to empirically confirm or disconfirm the "ideal" laws of consumer behavior.

This state of affairs becomes even more apparent if we take our data from a group of actual consumers who, as is almost inevitably the case in any real sample of data, differ in their tastes, their incomes, and their preference scales. In this case the data of the group's purchases do not reflect directly the preferences of each member of the group. Instead the data represent some other aggregation of their preference scales. To proceed to use these data to test the "ideal" laws is simply impossible, since the theory of demand gives one no rules for interpreting the behavior of assorted preference scales. The only possible approach is to view this data as being generated by some "representative" consumer. Yet, to do this is to place the problem in exactly the same predicament as before. The data can tell us which commodities this "representative" consumer actually chose; and the theory cannot tell us which commodities he should have chosen. To be able to do so the theory would have to have a large number of interpretive rules so that the experimenter could determine in each case the set of behavior patterns that would be consistent with the "ideal" law. Without these rules the "ideal" laws of behavior cannot be tested. The theory of utility, therefore, must be classified as an uninterpreted theoretical structure that is incapable of being refuted by empirical test.

B. Testing the Theory of Demand

In the previous section we have shown that the basic postulates of utility theory cannot in their present state be empirically confirmed. Consequently, the theory of utility is not refutable by empirical test. Since the concepts of the theory of demand depend for their empirical content on the empirical validity of utility theory, it would also appear that the theory of demand is not subjectable to a process of empirical confirmation. This conclusion is perfectly sound if the theory of utility and its basic postulates represent the only possible source of empirical content. If this is in fact the case, and our analysis in Chapter 4 seems to indicate that it is, then on the basis of our analysis so far we can conclude that the theory of demand is also an uninterpreted theoretical structure incapable of producing explanations and predictions of economic events.

Nevertheless, before we can accept this conclusion we must first examine the theory of demand in more detail to see whether it does not have its own sources of empirical content. If empirically testable relations can be discovered, then the theory of utility can derive its empirical content from the theory of demand. If this can be shown to be the case, then the non-testability of the basic postulates of utility theory will no longer prevent the theory of demand from being empirically confirmed.

To ascertain whether the theory of demand does in fact contain testable empirical relations we must abandon our examination of the basic postulates and focus our attention instead on the testability of the derived laws. Since the theory of demand has only one major consequence, we must now turn our attention to the demand functions themselves or what is sometimes called the Law of Demand.

As noted earlier, the demand function for the ith consumer, for commodity x_j, is expressed in terms of the prices of all other commodities and his income. This is represented by the expression:

$$D_{ij}(x_j) = f_{ij}(p_1, p_2, \ldots, p_n, y_i)$$

This function is expressed in terms of the ith consumer's demand for a certain commodity x_j. However, since we have already seen the type of difficulties that are encountered when the behavior of particular individuals is considered, let us first examine the case where the demand function is rewritten so that it represents the demand for commodity x_j of a particular group of consumers. From various empirical studies of demand it is clear that a group demand function can be constructed. This demand function represents and relates the purchases of x_j as a function of the prices of the other commodities available and the group's income. It has also been shown that in most cases the demand function will have a negative slope and that its other properties will closely approximate those discussed in Chapter 3.[18] The question that must now be answered is whether or not this empirical relation represents a general law that has the standard universal and conditional form. If it does, we have succeeded in our search for an empirical law. If it does not, we must conclude that the theory of demand is not empirically testable, as there are no other empirical relations left to examine.

However, let us return for the moment to our empirically determined demand function. Can we show that it is one example of the general law of demand? To be able to do so will require us to show that certain properties of this law are universally true. One of these properties is that demand curves are always drawn with negative slopes. But empirical studies have discovered cases where the slope of the demand curve for a particular commodity is positive. Hence, if we are to take the negative slope as a universal property of demand curves, we must have a technique for identifying and excluding those commodities for which demand curves have a positive slope. Now in Chapter 3, we saw that the slope of the demand curve—that is, the rate of change of the quantity of X demanded with respect to the price of X—was given by the Slutsky Equation:

$$\frac{\partial x}{\partial p_x} = \left(\frac{\partial x}{\partial p_x}\right)_{U=\text{constant}} - x\left(\frac{\partial x}{\partial y}\right)_{price=\text{constant}}$$

Further, it was pointed out that the term $(\partial x/\partial p_x)_{U=\text{constant}}$ the substitution effect, was always negative. From this it follows that $\partial x/\partial p_x$ is also negative unless the value of the income effect is such that

$$\left|- x\left(\frac{x}{y}\right)_{price=\text{constant}}\right| \geq \left|\left(\frac{x}{p_x}\right)_{U=\text{constant}}\right|$$

As a result, if we can identify those commodities for which a rise in price will induce a large and positive income effect, then we can place them to one side and state that our law of demand applies

---

[18] For particular examples of demand curves see the results presented by H. Schultz, *The Theory and Measurement of Demand*, University of Chicago Press, 1938; and for an excellent review of more recent research see: R. Ferber, "Research on Household Behavior," *American Economic Review*, Vol. **52**, March 1962, pp. 19–63.

to all other commodities but those. Yet the only means given to us by the theory of demand for identifying these special commodities is to note whether the slope of the demand curves is positive—that is, whether

$$\left| - x \left(\frac{\partial x}{\partial y} \right)_{price = \text{constant}} \right| \geq \left| \left(\frac{\partial x}{\partial p_x} \right)_{U = \text{constant}} \right|.$$

Since the substitution effect, $(\partial x/\partial p_x)_{U = \text{constant}}$ cannot be directly observed, it is not possible to independently measure its size, even if it were possible to directly measure the income effect. Thus, the slope of the demand curve for a particular commodity can only be discovered by observing the purchases made by a particular group of consumers. Also, since we cannot state that the preferences and tastes of consumers do not change over time, it is not possible to state that the demand curve for a particular commodity will always have a positive slope. If we cannot identify the commodities for which the law of demand does not apply prior to and independently of an empirical test of the law, then, as we have seen above, it is not possible to empirically disconfirm the law. For example, all the evidence that is collected in demand studies either agrees with the law—that is, the demand curves have a negative slope—or if the slopes are positive, then this result merely identifies at that point in time, those commodities to which the law does not apply. Therefore, the empirical studies of consumer demand can only support the law, never disconfirm it.

Moreover, if the basic postulates of utility theory were empirically confirmable then one could investigate the preferences and tastes of consumers and ascertain to what degree preferences for commodities changed with time. But the theory of utility does not provide sufficient interpretive rules to allow such conclusions to be drawn. Hence, we have no evidence to suggest whether a particular demand relation that exists at one period of time will continue to exist at some other period of time, even for the same group of consumers. For example, a particular demand function can be constructed for a particular set of commodities and prices during a specific time period. If, however, this demand function were then to be used during a different period of time to predict the amount purchased at a new price of the same commodity, the failure of this prediction could not be used to disconfirm the law. Unless we have independent evidence which strongly suggests that the relevant conditions—that is, those encompassed by the *ceteris paribus* conditions–have remained unaltered during the interval of time between these events, it cannot be argued that the parameter values determined during one period of time will apply to another.[19]

In this discussion we have taken the negative slope as one of the major properties of a demand curve. We could also have examined whether all demand functions were homogeneous of degree zero. Yet, if we cannot establish the negative slope as a universal property of demand curves there is no point in pursuing our investigation of the other properties any further. For if demand curves can have negative, positive, or possibly zero slopes, it does not help us establish an empirical law of demand to know whether they are homogenous of degree zero or not. Indeed the property of homogeneity can only be established after the law of demand has itself been empirically established. Thus, until it is possible to independently identify those commodities that are beyond the purview of the law; and until it is possible to demonstrate that a demand relation which exists at one period of time also holds at another period of time; it is not possible to empirically establish the law of demand. If we cannot establish the law of demand as an empirical generalization, then it follows that the theory of demand is virtually devoid of empirical content. Therefore, the theory of demand, like the theory of utility, must be classified as an uninterpreted theoretical structure that is incapable of being refuted by empirical test.

C. Explanations and Predictions with the Theory of Demand

In the first section of this chapter we deliberately emphasized the point that it was not possible to construct a scientific explana-

---

[19] Emile Grunberg in his paper, "Notes on the Verifiability of Economic Laws," *Philosophy of Science*, Vol. **24**, 1957, pp. 337–348, points out this difficulty in the following manner: "Sometimes the explanation of a unique event is said to make possible the prediction of a subsequent event. Let those events be E and E' respectively. Closer examination reveals that—regardless of whether there is an explanation of E—the prediction of E' simply uses observable attributes of E as initial conditions. Likewise the set [of general laws] L' used in the prediction of E' is independent from the set L which might be used in the explanation of E." (p. 339)

tion for the occurrence of an event unless at least one of the general laws contained in the explanation was an empirical law. In the following sections we examined the theory of utility and the theory of demand and discovered that both of these theories were uninterpreted theoretical structures and did not contain an empirical law. As a result, it is clear that the explanations of economic events that are offered by these theories cannot be scientific explanations. How then can we characterize them? To assist in our analysis of this question we shall make use of the following example of what would be a scientific explanation of an economic event.

Let the event to be explained E_T be an increase in the amount purchased, during a certain time period, of a particular commodity X_i by a specified group of consumers living in a particular geographic region. In order to establish an explanation for this event, we need to state the initial conditions and the general laws from which an increase in the demand for X_i can be deduced. The initial and boundary conditions could be given by the following observations: Commodity X_i is one of a number of commodities that are frequently purchased by the group of consumers under consideration. The prices and quantity consumed of all the commodities are known and it is observed that the price of commodity X_i has recently been lowered. Further, it is observed that these consumers regularly spend a certain percentage of their total income on these types of commodities. Now the set of general laws would consist of the following: A *quantitive* law relating the quantity purchased of commodity X_i to the prices of the other available commodities, as well as the percentage of the group's total income that is spent on these commodities. A law specifying precisely how consumers *should act* so as to maximize their utility from their purchases of available commodities.

From the initial and boundary conditions and these general laws, an increase in the amount of X_i purchased could be logically deduced. Further, if, prior to seeing whether the demand had actually increased, we had been asked to predict the change in the amount of X_i purchased, we would have been able to do so from a listing of the initial and boundary conditions and a statement of the relevant general laws.

In the previous sections we have pointed out that it is not possible to construct this type of an explanation from the currently accepted theory of demand. That it is not possible to do so is clear since neither the theory of utility nor the theory of demand contains the requisite empirical laws. However, events such as the one described above are frequently explained by economists in a manner that is quite similar to that which we have provided in our example. The principal difference between the scientific and the "economic" explanation is that the explanatory schemata of the latter cannot be used to generate testable predictions. Thus, it can only take the form of what we shall call an "explanatory rationalization" of the event after it has occurred. For example, the functional relation between price and the quantity purchased of X_i can be empirically determined only by observing the purchases that are actually made. Also the preferences and tastes of consumers can be determined only *after* they have decided which commodities to purchase out of the total number available to them. In a similar manner the reaction of consumers to a rise in price can be empirically determined only *after* the event has occurred; and except in the most simple of cases,[20] it is not known either before or after the event whether the consumers have in fact maximized their utility or not.

"Economic" explanations, then, are *ex post facto* rationalizations of the occurrence of the event under consideration. That is to say, the theories of utility and demand are sufficient to provide after-the-fact rationalizations of why an event occurred; but, as we have shown, they are not sufficient to produce an explanation of an event before it has occurred. In keeping with Papandreou's analysis[21] we shall classify this type of explanation as an *ex post facto* explanatory schema. Hence, we can conclude that until interpretive rules are discovered which permit general empirical laws to be developed, the explanations of consumer behavior offered by the theory of demand will remain ingenious rationalizations that must be classified under an *ex post facto* explanatory schema.

---

[20] Binary choice and other similar experiments.

[21] A. G. Papandreou, *op. cit.*, p. 139.

The Economist's Dilemma

In the previous two chapters we have submitted the theories of utility and demand to a fairly extensive examination. From our analysis of the function of their concepts and laws we have been led to the conclusion that neither the basic postulates nor the derived laws can be subjected to a process of refutation by empirical test. As we have seen, this implies that the theory of demand lacks empirical meaning and, therefore, cannot be employed to establish scientific explanations or predictions of consumer behavior. Since the theories of utility and demand play an important role in the formulation of a large part of micro-economic theory, it would appear by direct implication that many other parts of micro-economic theory are also not refutable by empirical test. If this is in fact the case, then this conclusion suggests that it is perhaps the economist's methodology that is at fault. Since the literature is somewhat replete with statements on how economists should go about the business of developing economic theory, the object of this chapter is not to increase by the number of articles devoted to that task. Rather our purpose is to re-examine the basic problems encountered in subjecting the theory of demand to empirical test, and from this investigation try to ascertain to what extent the methodological devices used by economists are responsible for this absence of predictability.

1. PREDICTION AS THE CRITERION OF EMPIRICAL VALIDITY

As noted in the Introduction, the history of economics is in part a history of a debate over the criteria that should be employed to adjudge the empirical validity of economic theory. This debate has primarily centered upon the basic postulates (or assumptions) of micro-economic theory. On one side it has been held that the truth value of the micro-theories should depend upon the empirical reality of the assumptions. Other economists were of the opinion that it did not matter whether these assumptions were descriptively realistic or not since at best they had to consist of abstractions from actual behavior. Their concern was only whether these abstract assumptions were sufficiently good approximations to observable behavior to serve as a reasonable basis for the theoretical constructions.[1] More recently it has been argued that, "Its [positive economics'] task is to provide a system of generalizations that can be used to make correct *predictions* about the consequences of any change in circumstances. Its performance is to be judged by the precision, scope, and conformity with experience of the *predictions* it yields."[2] Further, the debate over the reality of the assumptions is misconceived in that, ". . . the relevant question to ask about the 'assumptions' of a theory is not whether they are descriptively 'realistic,' for they never are, but whether they are sufficiently good approximations for the purpose in hand. This question can be answered only by seeing whether the theory works, which means whether it yields sufficiently accurate predictions. The two supposedly independent tests thus reduce to one test."[3] While this position is one which few economists appear willing to quarrel with, let us examine for a moment the implications of this criterion and the manner in which the prediction of an event is frequently employed in micro-economic analysis.

A. Implications of the Prediction Criterion

In the preceding chapter we briefly examined the function of general laws in the prediction of an event. We pointed out that their role in a predictive inference was similar to their function in a scientific explanation. It also was noted that the prediction of an event was frequently used as a means for subjecting a theory to a process of empirical confirmation. At this point, however, we wish to examine the logical structure of a prediction so that we can be in a better position to judge whether the successful prediction of an event is a sufficient criterion by which to judge the empirical truth value of micro-economic theory.

To facilitate this analysis we shall employ the notation employed

---

[1] Comments on this dispute can be found in the writings of J. S. Mill, *Essays on Some Unsettled Questions of Political Economy* (London School of Economics and Political Science, Reprint No. 7, 1948), especially pp. 143–149; and excellent examples can be found in the literature on the "marginalist controversy" in the *American Economic Review*, Vols. **36–38**, March 1946-June, 1948.

[2] Milton Friedman, *Essays in Positive Economics*, University of Chicago, 1953, p. 4. (Italics added.)

[3] *Ibid.*, p. 15.

in Chapter 2, Section 2, where the letters P, Q, R, S, are the names of variables in our metalanguage of deductive systems. If we let A and B be the names of the basic postulates (or assumptions) of a particular theory (an applied deductive system), and C the name of a general hypothesis that can be inferred from A and B, then we can let D be the name of a hypothesis that is inferred from the basic postulates and the hypothesis C. If we then let the variables of the metalanguage correspond to these statements in the object language, we can represent this sequence of inferences as follows:

$$P \cdot Q \to R \qquad \text{(from } P \text{ and } Q \text{ we can infer } R)$$

and

$$(P \cdot Q \to R) \to S \qquad \text{(from the expression}$$
$$P \cdot Q \to R \text{ we can infer } S)$$

Now let us suppose that we wish to test this theory by predicting the occurrence of an event and observing whether it does in fact occur in the prescribed manner. Furthermore, let our deduced law (or hypothesis) S be the predicted inference against which we shall compare the actual observations. Assume that the test is conducted, the event is observed, and we are now examining whether the data corroborate the statement S. Let us suppose, for the moment, that the answer is in the affirmative. The question that we wish to pose is, under what conditions does the empirical support for S provide empirical confirmation for P, Q, and R? For if the correct prediction of an event is to be the criterion by which we judge the empirical truth value of a theory, then we must be sure of the conditions under which there is a connection between confirmatory evidence for S and the theoretical structure composed of P, Q, and R.

In Chapter 2, Section 2, we also noted that if a theory was to be considered a part of empirical science, then it had to be possible to submit the theory to a process of refutation by empirical test. Hence, if we wish to empirically confirm the expression $P \to Q$, it is not sufficient to find evidence which supports Q; P must also be shown to be empirically true before the expression can be said to be confirmed.

Returning now to our predicted inference S, we can see that if we know that the empirical value for $(P \cdot Q \to R)$ is 'true', and we have data which supports S, then we can conclude that we have a confirming instance for $(P \cdot Q \rightarrow R) \rightarrow S$. In this case we could say that our theory has passed an empirical test by being able to correctly predict the occurrence of S. Conversely, if the evidence had not supported S, but we still had evidence suggesting that the empirical value for $(P \cdot Q \rightarrow R)$ was 'true', then we could conclude that the empirical value for the expression $(P \cdot Q \rightarrow R) \rightarrow S$ was 'false'. This then would be a case where the failure to correctly predict the occurrence of S would be sufficient to disconfirm at least one of the theory's hypotheses.

But now consider the case when we do not know the empirical truth value of the expression $(P \cdot Q \rightarrow R)$. Clearly, if the predicted event occurs the evidence supports the statement S. But to know only the empirical truth value for S does not allow us to determine the empirical truth value of the expression $(P \cdot Q \rightarrow R)$. Hence, if we are unable to determine the empirical truth value of $(P \cdot Q \rightarrow R)$, it is clearly not possible to use the evidence supporting the statement S to confirm or disconfirm the theory represented by the expression $(P \cdot Q \rightarrow R)$.

If we have some way of empirically determining the 'truth' or 'falsity' of P and Q—that is, if P and Q happen to be empirical laws—then we can test the empirical validity of both R and S. In this case any negative evidence will be sufficient to disconfirm them. Also, it should be noted that if R is an empirical law from which S can be deduced with the assistance of P and Q, then the knowledge that the empirical value of R is 'true' is sufficient to allow the expression to be confirmed or disconfirmed by empirical test.

From this analysis it is clear that the prediction of an event can only be employed as a means of testing a theory when some parts of the theory have already been well confirmed. This result corresponds directly with the requirements set out in Chapter 5 for a scientific explanation—namely, that the explanans must contain at least one empirical law. Since all theoretical structures do not necessarily contain well confirmed laws, we cannot conclude that the successful prediction of an event is a sufficient criterion by which to judge the empirical truth value of a theory.

B. Prediction and Micro-Economic Analysis

From our analysis of what we shall call the logic of prediction we can now see that if we are to be able to use the successful prediction of an event as confirmatory evidence, then the theory itself must already contain some parts that are empirically well confirmed. Thus, to return to the debate over the assumptions, either the basic postulates or some of the general laws contained in the theory must be accepted as empirically well-confirmed before it is possible to employ the evidence of a test prediction for any confirmatory purpose.

Consider, however, the following example of a position which has frequently been held by economists: "Consider the problem of predicting the shots made by an expert billiard player. It seems not at all unreasonable that excellent predictions would be yielded by the hypothesis that the billiard player made his shots *as if* he knew the complicated mathematical formulas that would give the optimum directions of travel, could estimate accurately by eye the angles, etc., describing the location of the balls, could make lightning calculations from the formulas, and could then make the balls travel in the direction indicated by the formulas. Our confidence in this hypothesis is not based on the belief that billiard players, even expert ones, can or do go through the process described; it derives rather from the belief that, unless in some way or other they were capable of reaching essentially the same results, they would not in fact be *expert* billiard players."[4] In order to clarify what it is that is being said here we shall employ our logical notation. Let D be the relation between the billiard balls described by the expert making his shot. Hence, D is the event that is described by the sentence "Consider the problem of predicting the shots made by an expert billiard player." And let C be "the hypothesis that the billiard player made his shots *as if* he knew the complicated mathematical formulas. . . ." By substituting variables for these sentences the theory can now be represented by the relation $R \rightarrow S$. But, we have just seen that the existence of evidence confirming S does not establish the empirical truth value of the expression $R \rightarrow S$, unless we have prior knowledge of the empirical truth value of R. Yet, in the passage quoted above we are asked to believe R merely because there is some evidence for S, not because we have any

---

[4] This example is taken from Friedman, *op. cit.*, p. 21 and can also be found in M. Friedman and L. J. Savage, "The Utility Analysis of Choices Involving Risk," *Journal of Political Economy*, Vol. **56**, August 1948; p. 298. (Reprinted in the A. E. R. *Readings in Price Theory*, Chicago, 1952.)

evidence in favor of R. In fact we are even informed that it would be highly unlikely for the empirical evidence to support R. Clearly, if we want $R \to S$ to be a testable empirical expression this approach is mistaken.

This is not to say that we cannot employ the procedure of assuming that the empirical value for R is 'true' and then examining the evidence in favor of S to see whether the relation $R \to S$ *could* be confirmed. If we find confirming evidence for S, then we know that if we can find confirming evidence for R that we will then be able to confirm the expression $R \to S$. But in the absence of any evidence pertaining to R, it is evident that we cannot establish the truth value of the empirical expression $R \to S$.

To examine one further point raised by this example we shall return for a moment to the hypothesis R which is stated in the following terms: "the billiard player made his shots *as if* he knew the complicated mathematical formulas . . .". We have already seen that if the expression $R \to S$ is to be capable of refutation by empirical test then the hypothesis R must be stated in such a way that it can be empirically confirmed. However, it frequently occurs in the statement of micro-economic theories that the principal postulates or hypotheses are stated in such a way that they cannot be disconfirmed. For example, the principal hypothesis in the theory of the firm is normally stated in the following manner: "That individual firms behave *as if* they were rationally seeking to maximize their expected returns." Typically, the evidence produced in favor of this hypothesis is the statement that if the behavior of firms were not consistent with this hypothesis then they would probably not be in business for very long. But here we are back to the problem of trying to confirm an expression like $R \to S$ by finding some evidence in favor of S. To empirically confirm the expression $R \to S$ we need to be able to test the hypothesis R. The inclusion of the *as if* clause in R does not matter as long as R is an empirically testable hypothesis. If the inclusion of the *as if* clause precludes the possibility of empirically testing R, then no matter how much evidence there is in favor of S we cannot conclude that the expression $R \to S$ has been empirically confirmed.

C. Prediction and Probabilistic Laws

Up to now our analysis of the problems involved in employing the prediction of an event to confirm a given body of theory has only been concerned with theories that contained general laws stated in the universal and conditional form. That is to say, we have only been considering theoretical structures in which the general laws, postulates and hypotheses have the following form: for every value of x_i all instances of $P(x_i)$'s are $Q(x_i)$'s. However, not all laws are stated in this form, and we shall now briefly turn our attention to the special problems that are encountered when the theoretical system contains laws, postulates, or hypotheses that are stated in probabilistic form.[5]

A hypothesis or law is stated in probabilistic form when it asserts that certain properties of various specified events are associated by a particular statistical frequency. For example, if we employ the notation given above, a simple probabilistic law would be given by the following: The probability that an occurrence of $P(x_i)$ will also be an occurrence of $Q(x_i)$ is given by r, where r represents the long-run frequency of all $P(x_i)$'s being $Q(x_i)$'s. Restating this law in more common statistical notation, we can represent it by the following: for all (x_i), $p[P(x_i), Q(x_i)] = r$. Examples of these laws abound in almost all the sciences, e.g., laws of quantum mechanics, genetics, psychology, etc., but perhaps are most frequently encountered in games of chance. Our concern here is not to justify the use of these laws but to examine the special character of the explanations and predictions in which they occur.

Consider the following example of a statistical explanation of the occurrence of a particular event. The event to be explained is the behavior of a subject involved in the binary choice experiment. The object of the experiment is to determine whether the subjects involved in the series of tests behave in a fashion that is consistent with a particular law of behavior. The law in question is a statistical law stating that a very high percentage of all subjects will behave so

---

[5] For a considerably more comprehensive analysis—to which this section is indebted—of the problems encountered when probabilistic laws are employed see: Carl G. Hempel, "Deductive-Nomological vs. Statistical Explanation," Part II, in H. Fiegl, *et al.* (eds.) *Minnesota Studies in the Philosophy of Science*, University of Minnesota Press, 1962, Vol. **III**.

as to maximize their expected utility. Assume that a specific subject is observed to behave in a manner that is consistent with the maximization of his expected utility. Accordingly the explanation for this event is given in the following way: Since almost all subjects behave in this experiment so as to maximize their expected utility, and since this particular subject does not differ in any significant sense from any of the other subjects, we can conclude that it was almost certain, or very likely, that this subject would behave so as to maximize his expected utility. It is apparent from this example that we cannot deduce from our law that this subject *will* act so as to maximize his expected utility. The best that we can do is assert that it is very likely that he will behave in this fashion.

Under this formulation it appears that a statistical explanation is really quite similar to what we have called a scientific explanation. It appears that we can still deduce the occurrence of the particular event. Upon closer examination, however, this apparent similarity disappears.

In a scientific explanation we employed a universal relation given by 'all P's are Q's'. We then observed that if a given event had the property P we were able to conclude that it also had the property Q.

But, in the case of a statistical explanation this is no longer true. For example, let us alter our law so that it now becomes "almost all P's are Q's"—that is, $p[P, Q] = r$, where r is the relative frequency, say, 0.95. We now observe the occurrence of an event, say X, and notice that it has the property P. Clearly we can no longer conclude that X will also have the property Q. On the contrary, since our statistical law only refers to "almost all" of the events of type X that have the property P, there are bound to be occurrences of the event X with the property P that do not have the property Q.

Even this situation would not cause us too much trouble if we could infer from our law the precise statistical probability with which events of type X having the property P also have the property Q. If this probability could be deduced from the statistical law then we would not have to restrict our conclusion to statements such as "it is very likely that this subject will behave in this fashion." On the contrary we could then deduce that "with a probability of q" this subject will behave so as to maximize his expected utility, where the term "probability" would refer to the normal frequency, or statistical, notion of probability. However, this conclusion cannot be made. The reason for this is that a statistical probability is not a property of an event or a statement but describes a relation that holds between two classes of events. In order to clarify this point let us examine once again our example of a statistical explanation. Our law is given by "almost all $P(x_i)$'s are $Q(x_i)$'s". Our observation is given the statement "event X has the property P". And we wish to determine the probability that we can attach to the statement "event X also has the property Q". Since the statement "event X also has the property Q" is the conclusion that we are after it is clear that it stands in some sort of relation to the two other sentences used in the explanans. Thus, if we are to know the statistical probability to attach to this conclusion we must know the statistical probability that characterizes the relation between the conclusion and the explanans. That is to say, somehow we need to be able to compute the probability that characterizes the relation between the sentence "event X also has the property Q" and the two other sentences "event X has the property P" and "almost all $P(x)$'s are $Q(x)$'s." But a statistical probability characterizes the relation between two classes of events. Therefore, it is not possible to deduce the desired statistical probability. At best, the desired probability can be represented by an inductive probability—a notion of probability that is distinctly different from the frequency or statistical notion.[6] Therefore, the only conclusion that can be drawn is that the occurrence of the sentence "event X also has the property Q" is very likely when taken in relation to the two sentences "event X has the property P" and "almost all $P(x)$'s are $Q(x)$'s."

Because we are unable to conclude any more than that the occurrence of Q is very likely, the logical character of the explanation or the prediction of $Q(x)$ is quite distinct from that which we have previously considered. Earlier we saw that if P was empirically

---

[6] For a more detailed discussion of the difference between inductive and statistical probabilities see: R. Carnap, "Statistical and Inductive Probability," in E. H. Madden (ed.), *The Structure of Scientific Thought*, Boston, 1960, pp. 269–278; and for a more extensive analysis of inductive logic see: R. Carnap, "On Inductive Logic," *Philosophy of Science*, Vol. 12, 1945.

confirmed, and our explanation could be characterized by the expression $P \rightarrow Q$, then the unsuccessful prediction of Q could be used to disconfirm the expression $P \rightarrow Q$. But if the law is stated as $p[P, Q] = r$, then no matter what evidence we have confirming P the unsuccessful prediction of Q cannot be used to disconfirm the law. Thus, the inclusion of probabilistic laws into the theoretical structure also precludes the possibility of employing the criterion of prediction as the sole means of confirming or disconfirming the derived relations.

2. OTHER APPROACHES TO EMPIRICAL VALIDATION

Since the successful prediction of the occurrence of an event can be used to empirically confirm or disconfirm the expression $R \rightarrow S$ only if the hypothesis R is also empirically confirmed, we shall now turn to an examination of the methods employed by economists to establish the empirical truth value of R. To facilitate this discussion we shall conduct this analysis in terms of the theory of demand allowing the reader to extrapolate the argument to the relevant portions of the remainder of micro-economic theory.

In Chapter 5, it will be remembered, we concluded that the derived laws of the theories of utility and demand were not capable of being directly refuted by empirical test because they lacked sufficient empirical interpretation. Employing the logic of prediction it then follows that neither the successful nor the unsuccessful prediction of an event can be used as evidence for the empirical truth value of these laws. If we cannot employ the technique of direct testing or that of prediction to confirm these laws we must now examine other suggested methods for establishing their empirical truth value.

A. Independent Confirmation

One possibility is to see whether a set of tests can be devised that will allow these laws to be subjected to a series of tests that are independent from their normal use in the explanation and prediction of economic events. If such a set of tests can be developed then not only will these laws be refutable by empirical test, but they will also confer empirical content on the explanations and predictions in which they are employed. Further, and what is more important, a body of laws will have been established that will assist in the determination of the empirical validity of other hitherto untested laws.

For example, in Chapter 5, Section 1, we presented an illustration of a scientific explanation. In that example three laws were explicitly mentioned: A quantitative law relating the change in pressure of water to its temperature and volume; a law stating the temperature at which water freezes given normal atmospheric pressure; and a law that stated how the pressure of a mass of water behaved when the volume was not allowed to increase and the temperature was lowered sufficiently to allow the water to freeze. Each of these laws can be subjected to a series of empirical tests that not only can be conducted independently from each other, but can also be performed independently from their use in the explanation of our particular event. Thus, when they are used together to establish the explanation of the cracking of the water container their own empirical validity ensures that the explanation has empirical meaning. Consequently, a prediction can be used to confirm or disconfirm particular hypotheses.

To be able to verify micro-economic laws independently from their use in explanations of economic events would imply that at least one of the two following conditions would have to be fulfilled: (i) that a series of tests could be established for the law of demand, or the law of maximization of utility, that was independent of the particular economic context in which it was used, (ii) that the law's parameter values determined by the data from one historic[7] event could then be directly applied to the explanation of another historic event.

The first condition implies that the empirical truth values of these laws must depend on the extent to which they are confirmed by the direct observation of human decision-making behavior. While this is not a novel conclusion it implies that psychological and other behavioral evidence must be taken into consideration when formulating and testing these laws. Consider, for example,

[7] The term "historic" is used to denote an event occurring during a particular time period and in a specified spatial location.

our previous reference to the binary choice experiment. In this experiment the choice situation is so structured that it is possible to determine at all times when the subject is behaving in a fashion that is consistent with the theory of utility that is being tested. If we let P and Q be variables representing the postulates of the theory and R a variable representing the derived law of utility maximization we can represent the theory by the expression $P \cdot Q \to R$. By repeating the experiment with a variety of subjects we can discover whether these subjects do in fact always behave in a fashion that is consistent with the behavior prescribed by R. That is to say, we can ascertain, in this situation, whether R is empirically confirmed or not. To be able to conclude that the expression $P \cdot Q \to R$ is also empirically confirmed we would have to separately gather evidence that supported the postulates P and Q. But, if we were testing the theory of utility in a normal situation it would no longer be possible to determine *beforehand* precisely what behavior patterns would be consistent with R. Hence, we would have to be able to confirm P and Q by separately observing the subject's decision-making behavior before any evidence in support of R could be used to help confirm the relation $P \cdot Q \to R$. In this case P and Q would have to represent postulates that were empirically confirmable by reference to some set of psychological or other behavioral evidence. In this way, the theory would be provided with empirical content and the empirical validity of $P \cdot Q \to R$ would be independent of a particular economic context.

If the second condition held it would mean that the data from one historic event would be sufficient to determine the law's parameter values which must now hold for a second historic event. In Chapter 5 we saw that this condition could be met if the law was formulated in terms of an ideal case. We noted that the law relating the free fall of bodies near the earth's surface to their acceleration is provided with sufficient interpretive rules so that the evidence from a particular test of this law can be used to confirm or disconfirm the ideal hypothesis. We then examined the derived laws of the theories of utility and demand to see whether these laws could be treated in a similar manner. It was discovered, however, that each of these laws contained at least one unidentified exogenous variable. The presence of unidentified exogenous variables, e.g., the wants and preferences of a consumer in the law of demand, implies that the set of events over which the law is supposed to hold cannot be completely defined or identified. Accordingly, there is an insufficient number of interpretive rules to allow one to determine whether the behavior of the consumer is consistent with the law or not. Until a sufficient number of interpretive rules is supplied it is not possible to employ the data gathered from one historic event to completely determine the parameters of the system. If the theoretical system cannot be completely determined at one instant of time, then it is not possible to assert that the parameter values determined from the data of this historic event should hold true for a second historic event. Thus, as the laws of the theories of utility and demand do not meet either of these two conditions we must conclude that it is not yet possible to independently establish the empirical validity of these laws.

B. Deduction from Empirically Valid Premises

So far we have seen that we cannot confirm the laws of the theories of utility and demand either directly or independently from their use in the explanation of economic events. The only alternative that remains is to examine whether these laws can be deduced from empirical premises. If these premises are formulated in such a way that they can be empirically confirmed, then the deduced laws will in turn become capable of refutation by empirical test, and the dilemma will be resolved. In the theory of demand these premises are represented by the basic postulates of the theory of utility. But we have already seen that it is not possible—except in a few heroically simplified cases—to subject these postulates to empirical tests. As in the case of the derived laws, the theory does not contain a sufficient number of interpretive rules to allow these ideal postulates to be directly compared with observable behavior. Yet, if we are to be able to subject the theory of demand to empirical tests these postulates must be interpreted so that they are capable of being directly confirmed by empirical test.

In this respect it is worth noting that many economists do not agree that it is necessary to subject these postulates (or assumptions as they are sometimes called) to empirical tests. On the contrary, these theorists argue that the postulates should be accepted as true without subjecting them to any tests. Further, they assert that it is only the laws that are deduced from these postulates that should be subjected to a process of empirical confirmation.[8] But we have already demonstrated that it is not possible to confirm these laws by direct tests. Consequently, the adoption of this position deprives micro-economic theory of any possible empirical content and of any interest to empirical science.

This is not to say that economics must be a part of empirical science. On the contrary, it has frequently been held that economics should be and in fact is an axiomatic discipline.[9] To accept this point of view implies, as we have already seen, that (a) the body of micro-economic theory cannot be used to establish scientific explanations or predictions of economic events, (b) the theory would be devoid of empirical content and hence policy prescriptions could not be based on any tested empirical laws, and (c) this axiomatic discipline should be renamed, perhaps meta-economics, so that there would be no confusion between the aims and interests of meta-economists and those who were concerned with developing theories to explain empirical phenomena.

The point at issue in this essay, though, is not whether economists should or should not become meta-economists. On the contrary, we have assumed for the purposes of this essay that micro-economics ought to be a part of empirical science. Clearly, it is this presup-

---

[8] For examples of this methodological approach to economic theory consider the following: "We do not need controlled experiments to establish their [the premisses'] validity; they are so much the stuff of our everyday experience that they have only to be stated to be recognized as obvious." Lionel Robbins, *An Essay on the Nature and Significance of Economic Science*, London, 2nd ed., 1935, p. 79. The numerous statements of this position found in the papers of the "marginalist controversy" in the *American Economic Review, op. cit.* And more recently, "Thus, the fundamental assumptions of economic theory are not subject to a requirement of independent verification, but instead to a requirement of understandability in the sense in which man can understand the actions of his fellow men." Fritz Machlup, "The Problem of Verification in Economics," *op. cit.*, p. 17.

[9] "What assigns economics its peculiar and unique position in the orbit of pure knowledge and the practical utilization of that knowledge is the fact that its particular theorems are not open to any verification or falsification on the ground of experience." Ludwig Von Mises, *Human Action: A Treatise on Economics*, Yale University Press, 1949, p. 33.

position that has led us through the foregoing analysis and up to the impasse we currently face.

Our goal is to employ the theory of demand to make testable predictions about consumer behavior. But our analysis has shown that it is not possible to do so. It is precisely this disparity between the objective and the performance that creates the dilemma facing economists today.

If we can abandon the goal of predicting behavior we can avoid the dilemma. But to adopt this policy is to ensure that the theory of demand will always remain empirically vacuous. A more attractive alternative is to resist retreat and apply our energies to discovering a way of overcoming it. And it is toward this objective that the remainder of this essay is devoted.

7

Toward a Set of
Testable Postulates

If the analysis in the preceding chapters is correct the dilemma facing micro-economic theory, and in particular the theory of consumer demand, can be summarized as follows:

(a) The derived laws of the theories of utility and demand contain unidentified exogenous variables customarily to be found in the *ceteris paribus* clause. These laws can neither be confirmed nor disconfirmed by empirical test.

(b) The derived laws could be empirically confirmed if and only if the basic postulates were empirically confirmed.

(c) The basic postulates do not contain a sufficient number of interpretive rules to permit them to be empirically confirmed.

(d) To be able to establish scientific explanations and predictions of economic events the laws of the theories of utility and demand must be formulated so that they can be subjected to a process of refutation by empirical test.

To state the problem, however, is not to solve it, even though an explicit statement of a problem is a necessary first step towards its solution. But it is frequently the case that the formulation of a problem itself provides clues as to the possible direction in which a solution may be found. And our dilemma does not appear to be an exception to this rule.

Our analysis has revealed that one way of turning theoretical structures into empirically testable theories is to develop a set of basic postulates from which fully identified laws can be deduced. Hence, if we are to convert the theory of demand into an empirically testable theory, one approach is to construct some testable postulates from which either the current or a revised theory of demand can be directly inferred.

If a new set of postulates is to be constructed that can be corroborated[1] by empirical tests this implies, as we have seen, that they must be formulated in such a way that they can be subjected to tests that are independent of a particular economic context. Consequently, if we are to be able to confirm these postulates inde-

---

[1] In the remainder of this essay the term "corroborate" will be used as a synonym for the term "confirm."

pendently of a specific economic context, then it would appear that they must be tested by direct reference to a fairly wide range of observable behavior. This train of reasoning suggests that the construction of these testable postulates would require a fairly close inspection of individual decision-making behavior. It would also appear to suggest that these postulates would then form the basis for a theory of individual decision-making behavior, which in turn would act as the empirical basis for the theories of utility and demand.

We are suggesting, therefore, that a possible solution to our dilemma can be found by first constructing a theory of individual consumer behavior. This theory must be a testable theory of behavior, and hence must be based and tested upon a wide variety of decision-making behavior. The second step is to employ the theory of individual consumer behavior as the empirical basis for the theories of utility and demand. If this procedure is to succeed the current theories of utility and demand will have to be revised to accommodate such new concepts and relations as are introduced by the underlying theory of decision-making behavior. In effect, we are suggesting that a solution to our dilemma lies in "reducing" the theories of utility and demand to a testable theory of individual consumer behavior.

So far in this essay we have not explored the practical or the theoretical possibility of formulating such a theory of decision-making behavior. But before we turn our attention to this problem we shall first examine the process of "reduction" alluded to above. Our object is to delimit the basic requirements that a theory of decision-making must meet if it is to form an empirical basis for the current theories of utility and demand—that is, if the theories of utility and demand are to be "reduced to" a theory of individual consumer behavior.

1. ON THE THEORY OF REDUCTION[2]

The term "reduction" is usually employed in science to denote the process whereby one branch of science, say chemistry, is reduced

---

[2] This section is principally indebted to E. Nagel's paper, "The Meaning of Reduction in the Natural Sciences," *Science and Civilization*, R. C. Stauffer (ed.), University of Wisconsin Press, 1949, pp. 99–135.

to another branch of science, say physics. What is meant by the term can briefly be characterized as follows: the reduction of chemistry to physics is said to have taken place if it is possible to formulate a theory involving only the terms of physics that is sufficient to explain all the phenomena that are explained by chemical theories. That such a reduction of one branch of science to another is considered to be desirable is evinced by the economy introduced into the theoretical vocabulary. If all phenomena in chemistry are explainable in terms of physical theories and observations recorded in physical terms, then all special terms previously contained in chemical theories may be put to one side and replaced by the appropriate physical terms. Needless to say, this economy is only achieved if the resulting physical theory has not been unduly increased in complexity and does not require a large number of special assumptions to allow the reduction process to take place.

For our purposes, however, we wish to consider another, and less frequently noted, application of the reduction process. The process we wish to consider is one in which a body of theory within a particular branch of science is replaced by a new theory that not only explains all the phenomena covered by the first theory but also a further set not covered by the previous theory at all. This is the process of reduction within a given branch of science. It can be more formally characterized as follows: Let T_1 represent the new and more comprehensive theory, and let T_2 represent the original and less comprehensive theory. Then the reduction of T_2 to T_1 is said to have occurred if and only if:

"(1) The vocabulary of T_2 contains terms not in the vocabulary of T_1.

(2) Any observational data explainable by T_2 are explainable by T_1.

(3) T_1 is at least as well systematized as T_2."[3]

It is important to note that this process of reduction characterizes, within a particular branch of science, the process of develop-

[3] P. Oppenheim and H. Putnam, "Unity of Science," *Minnesota Studies in the Philosophy of Science*, University of Minnesota, Vol. II, 1958, p. 5. Note that the term "systematized" is introduced and its meaning in relation to theories is explained in: J. G. Kemeny and P. Oppenheim, "Systematic Power," *Philosophy of Science*, Vol. 22, 1955, pp. 27–33.

ing new and more comprehensive theories. Also it should be noted that the development of the theory T_1 frequently entails a process whereby T_1 is based upon a set of data and postulates that are at a more microscopic level than those employed by the previous body of theory, T_2. In other words the process of reducing T_2 to T_1 and, consequently the process of developing the new and more comprehensive theory, T_1, frequently depends upon the existence of a body of data that is at a more microscopic level than that employed by T_2. For without the incentive provided by a more detailed level of data it is unlikely that T_1 would even be constructed. Hence, the reduction of T_2 to T_1 usually takes place after a set of relevant data which are at a more microscopic level than the data explained by T_2 has been discovered.

For example, consider the theoretical developments in physics that may be characterized by the meanings that can be given to the concept of temperature. First consider what is usually meant by the concept of temperature when a subject is presented with a mercury thermometer and is asked to determine the temperature of a particular container of water. After immersing the lower part of the thermometer in the water and allowing the mercury column to come to rest, the subject could be expected to state that the temperature of the water was, say, 20°C. If this subject was then asked to explain why it is that he can measure the temperature of water with the mercury thermometer, he might invoke the physical theory relating the volume expansion of mercury in a closed tube to the temperature of a body placed in contact with the mercury tube. If the antecedent conditions and the properties of the mercury column were properly specified he would have established an explanation of what he meant by the fact that the temperature of the water was 20°C. But, if we asked our subject to measure the temperature of substances that were either extremely hot or cold he would find that the mercury thermometer would not longer be sufficient to establish explanations. The mercury would either be vaporized or in a solid state. One alternative would be to construct explanations for these extreme temperatures in terms of other measuring instruments and the theories they invoke, e.g., thermocouples, pyrometers, and bolometers. But another alternative would be to turn to a more comprehensive theory of physics—namely, the kinetic theory of matter—where the temperature of a substance is expressed as the mean kinetic energy of the molecules of which the substance consists. In either event the theory that is invoked takes as its basic data phenomena that are microscopic when compared to the data employed in the theory invoked earlier to explain the behavior of the mercury column. What in effect has happened is that the laws of thermodynamics have been reduced to the laws of the kinetic theory of matter. What were once the basic postulates of the theory of thermodynamics are now the derived laws of the kinetic theory of matter.

Before we proceed to examine whether the basic postulates of the theories of utility and demand can be derived from some empirically testable micro-theory, we must first consider what is formally required before we can state that one theory has been successfully reduced to another.

The first condition follows directly from what we have stated is the objective of the reduction process—that is, to show that the laws and postulates of T_2 are directly deducible from the laws and postulates of the new theory T_1. If the laws or postulates of T_2 contain terms and expressions that do not appear in T_1, then it is clear that we cannot directly deduce T_2 from T_1. In this case various assumptions or further postulates must be introduced to link the terms in the derived laws of T_1 to the terms and expressions of T_2. For example, in our discussion of the various ways in which the concept of temperature could be explained we pointed out that one explanation could be given by using the laws of thermodynamics and the properties of the mercury column, while another could be given by employing the kinetic theory of matter. The concept of temperature occurs directly in the laws of thermodynamics. But it does not occur at all in the statement of the kinetic theory of matter. Thus, if we are to claim that the theory of thermodynamics has been reduced to the kinetic theory of matter some way must be found for linking the concepts of the kinetic theory to the concepts in the theory of thermodynamics. In actual practice this obstacle is overcome by the introduction of the assumption that the thermodynamic concept of temperature is directly proportional to the kinetic theoretic concept of the mean kinetic energy of the molecules. With the addition of this assumption the laws of thermodynamics can now be inferred from the kinetic theory of matter. From this discussion we can see that a necessary condition for the reduction of

T_2 to T_1 is that suitable relations be constructed so that the terms and expressions contained in T_2 are derivable from the basic postulates and concepts of T_1.

Another condition that must be met, if we are to consider T_2 to have been successfully reduced to T_1, is that the basic postulates or principal hypotheses of T_1 must be empirically testable as well as being reasonably well confirmed by the available evidence. The purpose of this condition is to ensure that we do not construct essentially trivial reduction theories. It would not be an important scientific accomplishment merely to construct a set of postulates from which T_2 could be deduced, if we were then unable to test or empirically confirm them. Therefore, before we can accept a theory, say T_1, as a possible basis for the reduction of T_2 we must be sure that the postulates or principal hypotheses of T_1 are both testable and reasonably well confirmed.

The condition of being "reasonably well confirmed" is admittedly vague. And, as has been pointed out earlier, the problems involved in determining the degree of confirmation go beyond the scope of our analysis. However, it is clear that a striking confirmation of these hypotheses takes place if hitherto unknown relations between observable phenomena are both deducible from the theory and supported by the available evidence. Further confirmation is supplied if the deduced relations of T_1 are actually in better agreement with the data explained by T_2 than the original relations contained in T_2. While these conditions do not define the degree to which a theory is confirmed they do provide important evidence that the empirical support for T_1 is greater than that which had been found for T_2.

From this discussion it is evident that the reduction of one body of theory to another cannot be said to have taken place unless the principal hypotheses of the new theory are tested and confirmed independently of the original theory. Further, when discussing the reduction of T_2 to T_1 the state in which these two theories are presented is also very important. That is to say, it must be demonstrated that the relations and deduced laws of T_2 are derivable from the new theory T_1. Also it should be noted that even though it is demonstrated that T_2 is reducible to T_1 this does not automatically invalidate the laws, concepts and postulates of T_2. On the contrary, the reduction of T_2 to T_1 may in effect strengthen the empirical confirmation of T_2, even though some of the laws of T_2 may appear to be only approximations to the more highly confirmed and precise laws of T_1.

2. ON REDUCTION AND A THEORY OF HUMAN DECISION-MAKING

Having outlined the theory of, and the conditions under which, the reduction of one theory to another is said to have taken place, we shall now return to the task of determining whether we can construct a theory that will serve as a basis for a micro-reduction of the theories of utility and demand. As noted earlier, it appears that if we are to be able to successfully reduce the theories of utility and demand, then the reducing theory will have to be a theory of individual decision-making behavior. While this is not a novel conclusion[4] it implies that we should begin our search for the postulates of our reduction theory among the recent researches in behavioral theories[5] and the simulation of individual decision-making behavior.[6] In spite of the fact that these researches are not all concerned with explaining the same economic events, they all employ a set of basic hypotheses that assert certain regularities in the decision-making process of economic actors. But before it is worth inspecting these theories to see if they can serve as the basis for our reduction

---

[4] For example, Emile Grunberg, *op. cit.*, p. 347, pointed out both the desirability and the possibility of reducing economic theory to psychological or behavioral terms.

[5] The most notable of the early researches in behavioral theories can be found in: R. M. Cyert and J. G. March, "Organizational Structure and Pricing Behavior in an Oligopolistic Market," *American Economic Review*, Vol. 45, 1955, pp. 129–139, and R. M. Cyert, E. A. Feigenbaum and J. G. March, "Models in a Behavioral Theory of the Firm," *Behavioral Science*, Vol. 4, April 1959, pp. 81–95; also for a detailed presentation of a new theory of the firm see: R. M. Cyert and J. G. March, *The Behavioral Theory of the Firm*, Prentice-Hall, Englewood Cliffs, 1963.

[6] For a survey of recent research in the simulation of decision-making behavior see the papers presented by G. H. Orcutt, M. Shubik, and G. P. E. Clarkson and H. A. Simon in "Simulation: A Symposium," *American Economic Review*, Vol. 50, Dec. 1960, pp. 894–932. For a more extensive analysis of the problems of simulating human decision-making behavior see: A. Newell and H. A. Simon, "The Simulation of Human Thought," *Current Trends in Psychological Theory*, University of Pittsburgh Press, 1961, pp. 152–179.

theory we need to examine the theory of individual decision-making behavior from which these theories have evolved.

A. A Theory of Human Problem Solving

The theory of human problem solving that we shall consider was developed by Newell, Shaw, and Simon[7] to explain and predict the performance of a human problem solver handling various specified tasks. The object of the theory is to explain the process of human problem solving by identifying the types of decision processes that humans employ while solving a variety of problems. Although questions about decision-making could be answered at various levels and in varying amounts of detail, this theory explains problem solving behavior in terms of a set of basic information processes. These processes are in part defined by the theory's three basic postulates which state that there exists for each problem solver:

"(1) A control system consisting of a number of *memories* which contain symbolized information and are interconnected by various ordering relations . . .

(2) A number of *primitive information processes*, which operate on the information in the memories . . .

(3) A perfectly definite set of rules for combining these processes into whole *programs* of processing. . . ."[8]

To further clarify what is meant by these postulates consider the following example of an application of these postulates that is contained in a recently proposed theory of trust investment behavior.[9] This theory of investment behavior was developed to explain and predict the portfolio selection process of a particular trust investor. The basic postulates of the theory state that for the trust investor there exist:

"(1) A *memory* which contains lists of industries each of which has a list of companies associated to it. The memory also

---

[7] A. Newell, J. C. Shaw, and H. A. Simon, "Elements of a Theory of Human Problem Solving," *Psychological Review*, Vol. **65**, No. 3, 1958, pp. 151–166.
[8] *Ibid.*, p. 151.
[9] G. P. E. Clarkson, *Portfolio Selection: A Simulation of Trust Investment*, Prentice-Hall, Englewood Cliffs, 1962.

contains information associated with the general economy, industries and individual companies. [Investors categorize companies by industry. Not all investors may associate identical companies with a given industry, but the process of classification by industry remains invariant as the primary basis for listing companies in the memory. The information associated with each company also varies among investors, but each may be represented as having a list of attributes with their values stored in memory, e.g., growth rate, dividend rate, price earnings ratio, expected earnings, expected yield, etc.]

(2) *Search* and *selection* procedures which perform the task of searching the lists of information stored in memory, selecting those items that have the required attributes, regrouping the selected pieces of information into new lists, and performing algebraic operations when necessary. These procedures function in a manner similar to that of the traditional clerk who prepares lists of stocks suitable for current investment by scanning a master list.

(3) A *set of rules* or criteria which guide the decision-making process by stipulating when and how each process is to be used. The set of rules constitutes the structure of the decision process for an individual investor. It might be compared to the heuristics of the traditional "expert," but as previously noted, there is an important difference—namely, the set of rules must be defined unambiguously."[10]

As can be seen from this example, it is a basic assumption of the theory of human problem solving that decision processes can be isolated as well as identified. And, further, that they can be represented by a series of straightforward mechanical processes. This is not to say that decision processes are simple or easy to represent. But rather that they can be broken down into their elemental parts, e.g., the memory, the search and selection procedures, and the rules for combining these processes, which in turn consist of collections of simple mechanisms. When these operations are recorded in a set of statements that describe the decision behavior of the individual

---

[10] *Ibid.*, p. 27.

under investigation, this set of rules becomes the theory of the individual's decision-making process. That this set of rules can be considered to be a theory is evidenced by the requirement that it must be possible to deduce unequivocally the externally observable behavior that will be generated from it. In order to ensure that this condition is met, the set of postulates and statements is translated into a computer language and tested on a digital computer. Thus, as in the more familiar case of our scientific theories, the logical consequences are derived by performing the particular operations according to the specified rules. In an actual test the behavior generated by the theory is compared with the observed decision behavior of the individual under consideration. When the rules and postulates for processing the information yield results that are consistent with those obtained from the human subject, the theory is said to be sufficient to account for the observed behavior. Hence, the theory of human problem solving establishes a theory of decision behavior by providing a basic set of postulates and hypotheses that when appropriately interpreted are asserted to be sufficient to generate the observed behavior.

B. On Testing the Hypothesized Relations

From our earlier discussion it was clear that if we were to employ a set of postulates as the basis of our reduction theory then these postulates must be independently confirmable by empirical test. In the event that we are to be able to reduce the theories of utility and demand to some new theory of decision-making behavior then these postulates must also be well confirmed. However, we are primarily concerned with discovering whether it is possible to carry out this reduction process. Hence, it will be sufficient for our purposes if we can show that the basic postulates of human problem solving are confirmable independently from a particular economic context.

In order to facilitate this analysis we shall make use of the following example of an explanation of an economic event that is proposed by the theory of trust investment mentioned above.

The event to be explained consists of the selection of a specific portfolio of securities by a particular trust investor for a specified trust account. To establish an explanation for this event the theory requires that the initial and boundary conditions $(O_1\tau_1, O_2\tau_2, \ldots,$

$O_n\tau_n$) include: Data on the historical, current, and expected values of relevant financial attributes, e.g., price, yield, earnings per share, etc., for a specified list of securities. Data on the historical, current and expected values of specified industrial and economic indices, and data on the particular trust account in question. The basic postulates of the theory, as noted above, specify that the trust investor can be represented as having: (i) a memory which contains the data given above listed in a particular form, (ii) a set of procedures that allow the data in the memory to be searched, manipulated, and desired pieces selected for further processing, and (iii) a set of decision rules that determine the decision-making process by stipulating when and where each decision process is to be applied. These postulates are concerned with the trust investor's decision procedures and they define both the structure and the order in which the decision processes are carried out.[11] When they are employed in conjunction with the initial and boundary conditions ($O_1\tau_1$, $O_2\tau_2$, ..., $O_n\tau_n$) they allow the decision process to be carried through and a particular portfolio of securities to be selected. Consequently, the explanation of the selection of a particular portfolio is established by applying the decision procedures specified by the theory to the data of the security market and of the particular trust account in question.

If we were interested in ascertaining whether this theory of trust investment could be suitably amended to serve as the basis for a micro-reduction of a theory of investment we should first want to determine whether this explanation was a scientific explanation or not. To decide this question we need to examine the postulates to see either if they are refutable by empirical test within their economic context, or if they can be corroborated independently from their use in the explanation of portfolio selections. If either of these conditions holds, it will be remembered, we are able to conclude that the theory has established a scientific explanation for this economic event. If both of these conditions hold the would be strong evidence in favor of the hypothesis that the theory of trust investment could be used as the basis for reducing the economic theory of investment to a testable theory of investment decision-making behavior.

---

[11] It should be noted that these postulates and decision rules are stated in sufficient detail to permit their programming and testing on a digital computer.

Clearly we are primarily interested in discovering whether these postulates can be tested independently of their economic context. But, if it can be shown that they are also capable of being refuted within their economic context, then this evidence would support the hypothesis that the basic postulates of the theory of human problem solving could also be used as the basis for a micro-reduction of the theory of demand. Therefore, we shall first examine whether it is possible to directly corroborate the postulates of the theory of trust investment.

The theory of trust investment was developed to explain and predict the portfolio selections of a particular trust investor. It was constructed by incorporating into the theory such decision mechanisms as were observed (and inferred) from the trust investor's behavior. To test the theory's ability to reproduce the decision behavior the theory was given the data of the security markets and of some specified trust accounts for a particular period of time. It was then required to generate portfolios for these trust accounts. But the specific portfolio selections constitute only the final result of the trust officer's decision process. Hence, the theory was also subjected to a set of tests that compared the behavior generated by its decision mechanisms with the recorded behavior of the trust investor.

In the actual testing program the theory was submitted to a series of these tests. In fact both the theory's portfolio selections and its decision processes were compared with those of the trust investor's on four separate occasions over a period of nine months.[12] Despite the fact that it is of some interest to be able to predict the actual portfolio selections of a particular trust investor, there are presumably a variety of theories that will permit this result to be accomplished. What is of greater importance, is the fact that the theory's generated decision behavior compared favorably with the observed decision behavior of the trust investor—that is to say, it appeared, even on close inspection, that the theory was employing many of the same decision procedures and was arriving at the same results for substantially the same reasons as the particular trust

---

[12] For a detailed presentation of the empirical tests and the results obtained from this testing procedure see: *Ibid.*, Chapters 5 and 6.

investor under investigation.[13] By comparing the behavior generated by each of the theory's important mechanisms directly with
the observed behavior of the trust investor it was possible to submit
the theory's decision processes to a direct process of refutation by
empirical test. Manifestly, this testing procedure is capable of being
repeated. Also the theory's decision processes are capable of being
compared with observed behavior to whatever level of detail is
desired. Hence, while the theory of trust investment may or may
not have been adequately confirmed, it is apparent that it is quite
possible to corroborate both its postulates and its generated hypotheses.

Having concluded that the theory's postulates are testable
within their economic context, we shall now examine whether they
can also be empirically confirmed independently from their use in
the explanation of economic events. Theories of individual decision-
making behavior are concerned with explaining various aspects of
human problem solving behavior. Also their postulates make definite assertions about the structure and ordering of certain decision
processes. Therefore, it is both in principle and in practice possible
to study human decision-making behavior independently of a particular economic context. For example, the decision-making behavior of individuals engaged in the solution of problems in geometry, logic, or chess,[14] to mention but a few examples, can be used as
the basis from which to test the empirical validity of many of the
hypothesized decision processes. This is not to say that all the hypotheses of a theory, say the theory of trust investment, can be
tested in this manner. Obviously, some of them, e.g., the order in

---

[13] For the results of the direct tests of the theory's decision mechanisms see:
Ibid., Chapter 7.

[14] It is worth noting that the decision processes employed in the theory of trust
investment were principally derived from researches in human problem solving
that used the problems of geometry, logic and chess as their sources of empirical
evidence. See for example: A. Newell, J. C. Shaw, and H. A. Simon, "Empirical
Explorations of the Logic Theory Machine," *Proceedings of the Western Joint
Computer Conference*, Feb., 1957, pp. 218–230, and "Chess-Playing Programs
and the Problem of Complexity," *IBM Journal of Research and Development*,
Oct., 1958, pp. 320–335; and H. L. Gelernter, J. R. Hansen, and D. W. Loveland, "Empirical Explorations of the Geometry Theorem Machine," *Proceedings of the Western Joint Computer Conference*, 1960, pp. 143–159.

which companies are listed in the memory, the order in which the testing and selecting of securities is performed, etc., will be peculiar to the particular economic context. What we are asserting is that a certain number of invariances exist in the decision processes of different problem solvers, and that it is possible to determine their empirical truth value. For example, the theory of human problem solving contains three main postulates which assert the existence in a human decision-maker of a memory, some primitive information processes, and a hierarchy of decision rules. The theory of trust investment turns these postulates into testable hypotheses by specifying in detail the content of the trust officer's memory and information processes as well as the content and order of his decision rules. If it was not possible to specify how to characterize these processes, then it would not be possible to directly adopt these postulates into a theory of investment behavior. In effect, we are arguing that unless invariances, like the structure of the contents in memory, exist between problem solvers, then it is not possible to construct a theory of human problem solving in this manner.

It should be noted, however, that the hypotheses of several theories of decision-making behavior[15] are directly derived from the basic postulates of the theory of human problem solving. Consequently, it appears that the empirical truth value of these postulates can be determined by a series of tests in a variety of empirical contexts. Also it should be noted that we are not asserting that all the hypotheses employed in these theories have been subjected to such a series of tests, but rather that it is in principle possible to do so and that our references to the literature contain examples where such a program is already being carried out.

For the purposes of our analysis, therefore, it it sufficient to demonstrate that it is possible to carry out such a testing pro-

---

[15] For examples of these theories see: E. A. Feigenbaum, "The Simulation of Verbal Learning Behavior," *Proceedings of the Western Joint Computer Conference*, Vol. 19, May 1961, pp. 121–132; J. Feldman, "Simulation of Behavior in the Binary Choice Experiment," *Proceedings of the Western Joint Computer Conference*, Vol. 19, May 1961, pp. 133–144. (Both of these papers are reprinted in E. A. Feigenbaum and J. Feldman (eds.), *Computers and Thought*, McGraw-Hill, 1963); and A. Newell, J. C. Shaw and H. A. Simon, "A General Problem Solving Program for a Computer," *Computers and Automation*, Vol. 8, July 1960, pp. 10–17.

cedure.[16] Because, if we assume for the moment that the appropriate empirical tests are performed, and that some of these postulates are not disconfirmed, then these postulates will have become independently tested empirical hypotheses and the solution to our dilemma will be in sight.

At this point it might be asked that even if we accept the proposition that certain hypothesized decision processes can be empirically confirmed, in what manner does this alter the essentially *ad hoc* character of these decision-making theories? After all, decision-making theories no less than current micro-economic theories are concerned with explaining and predicting historic events, and are constructed and amended to fit the data of particular events.

To argue in this fashion, however, is to disregard one very important point. By demonstrating that specific postulates about human problem solving behavior can be empirically confirmed we have turned the original postulates about human behavior into empirical hypotheses. Once we have a set of confirmed hypotheses all hypotheses that can be deduced from them become in turn capable of being, at least indirectly, confirmed or disconfirmed by empirical test. Hence, while a particular theory, say the theory of trust investment, may be employed in the explanation of a particular economic event, the independent testability of its basic hypotheses ensures that a scientific explanation has been established.

As we have already seen, what is true for a scientific explanation is also true for a scientific prediction. In other words, once some of the postulates have been established as empirical hypotheses, the prediction of the occurrence of an event can now be used as a basis from which to test the remainder of the hypotheses in the theory. For example, the trust investment theory was tested by requiring it to predict, under varying market conditions, the trust officer's portfolio selections. The predicted portfolios can be used to determine whether the decision mechanisms employed in the theory are sufficient to permit the changing economic conditions to be reflected in the securities that are selected. If the predicted port-

---

[16] The reader will note that we have repeatedly stated that it is not necessary for the purposes of this essay to examine the problems involved in ascertaining the degree of confidence in which a given hypothesis or theory is held.

folios compare favorably with the trust officer's at one period of time but not at another, then it would follow that the decision processes were not sufficient to allow the theory to adapt its selections to the prevailing market conditions.[17] Therefore, to the extent that empirical laws of decision-making behavior can be established we can then develop a body of decision-making theory that will have the same explanatory and predictive power as is enjoyed by other scientific theories.

CONCLUSIONS

At the beginning of this chapter we arrived at the conclusion that if we were able to resolve the dilemma facing the theories of utility and demand, we would first have to be able to construct a testable theory of individual decision-making behavior. We then demonstrated that it is possible to construct such a theory. And further that a certain amount of research in this direction has already been completed. As a result, we are now faced with the problem of trying to show how the theories of utility and demand are to be reduced to a theory of decision-making behavior. But the required reduction theory just does not exist. Hence, our task will be to explore the manner in which such a theory might be developed, as well as the structure that it might be expected to have. The object of this exercise is to provide the interpretive links between a theory of decision-making behavior and the theory of demand. And it is toward this goal that the next chapter is directed.

---

[7] The evidence on the theory's ability to adapt to changing market conditions is presented in *ibid.*, Chapter 6.

Toward a Testable Theory of Demand

In the previous chapter we have attempted to demonstrate that it is possible to develop a set of empirical hypotheses that can serve as the basis for a testable theory of individual decision-making behavior. Hence, if we are to reduce the theories of utility and demand to a theory of decision-making behavior, then it is clear that the reducing theory can be constructed so that it meets the first half of the second main condition. This condition requires the basic postulates or hypotheses of a reduction theory to be empirically testable. It is considerably less clear, without the theory being constructed and tested, that the second half of this criterion would be met—that is, that these hypotheses are also well confirmed. But this is a matter for empirical investigation. And it will be sufficient for our purposes to be concerned only with whether they can be considered to be empirically testable. Further, if the basis for the reduction process is to be a theory of human decision-making, then it would appear that statements would be deducible from this theory that would assert testable relations between observational phenomena that hitherto were not known. Since the basic theory would be empirically testable, and since researches into the simulation of human decision-making behavior have just begun, there appears to be a certain amount of *prima facie* evidence in favor of this conclusion. If this evidence can be accepted, for the time being, then it would appear that the reducing theory also meets the third condition that is imposed to adjudge successful theoretical reductions.

Given that a suitably constructed theory of decision-making behavior meets the last two conditions we must now examine whether it can pass the first and most important criterion—namely, whether the laws and postulates of the theories of utility and demand are directly deducible from the laws and postulates of the reducing theory. While the answer to this question is partly empirical—that is, do we have a theory that meets this test—it is the theoretical considerations that we shall be concerned with here. If the conditions for theoretically satisfying this criterion can be stated, and if it can be shown that a suitably constructed theory of decision-making behavior can meet these conditions, then our task will have been completed.

To build and test such a theory is a task for empirical research.

But to examine the conditions such a theory must meet, and to point to the various components that such a theory might have, is a task for theoretical and speculative analysis. And it is toward both of these latter objectives that this chapter is directed.

1. TOWARD A THEORY OF CONSUMER BEHAVIOR

Before we can determine whether the theory of demand can be reduced to a testable theory of decision-making behavior, we must have at least a general idea of the sorts of problems we are going to encounter. But in order to identify the types of problems this reduction process would entail we must first have a fairly clear idea of the kinds of behavior the theory of decision-making is going to explain, and the types of empirical statements that will be deducible from it. Thus, in order to begin to ascertain whether the theories of utility and demand are reducible to a theory of decision-making behavior, we must first construct, at least in general form, the theory that is to effect the reduction process.

To construct a theory, however, we need to have some knowledge about the events that the theory is supposed to explain. Do we wish to construct a theory that is designed to explain the behavior of particular individuals? Or is it the statistically average behavior of certain groups of consumers that we wish to be able to predict and and explain? Since we have based our approach to the dilemma on the possible solution offered by a testable theory of human problem solving, it would appear sensible to begin by developing a theory that closely parallels these empirical investigations. Consequently, we shall restrict our attention to the explanation of individual decision-making behavior.

In the event a testable theory of individual behavior is constructed that is sufficient to reduce the theories of utility and demand, we can then turn our attention to the problems of aggregation, and the task of constructing a more general theory of consumer behavior. But, we wish to be able to make use of such evidence as exists on the behavior of individual problem solvers. Thus we shall only consider the problem of developing a theory of decision-making behavior for an individual consumer. However, this need not be as restrictive as it may initally sound. It should not be forgotten that the theories of utility and demand were also originally constructed to explain the behavior of individual consumers.

From our earlier examination of these micro-economic theories we saw that they could be interpreted as "ideal" theories. That is to say, the theory of demand can be presented as a theory of "ideal" consumer behavior if a set of interpretive rules is provided so that the theory can be tested against the data of any particular case. It has also been noted that "ideal" theories or models are frequently employed in empirical science. Consequently, there appears to be a considerable amount of evidence in favor of approaching the problem in this manner. If we take the events to be explained as the decision-making behavior of individual consumers, then our task can be taken to be the construction of an "ideal" theory of consumer decision-making behavior which can be empirically interpreted to explain the behavior of a particular consumer.

The next question we must consider is the problem of where to begin. It is clear from our previous discussion that we are going to make use of the basic postulates of the theory of human problem solving. But these postulates are concerned with such things as the structure of memory and basic information processes. Thus, we must first have some idea of the particular way in which we wish to employ them before we will be able to specify their content in any detail. In order to be able to decide on the specific content these postulates should have, we should first examine some of the principal empirical statements that we shall want to be able to deduce once the theory has been built.

The first set of expressions is a decision process that allows the consumer to allocate his total income among the various categories, or groups, of available commodities, such as housing, food, clothes, entertainment, etc. The assumption would be that the decision to allocate funds among various categories of commodities, while not necessarily being made at one instant of time, is nevertheless a conscious decision process the consumer engages in over a period of time. If we also assume, for the moment, that our consumer belongs to a particular income group, then it is also quite reasonable to postulate that as long as his income keeps pace with his social and economic peers his allocative decision procedure will not vary a great deal from one period of time to the next. Now clearly these are postulates that are both empirically testable and for which a certain amount of evidence already exists.[1] In other words, we are postulating that: (a) each individual consciously decides over a period of time what proportion of his income to spend on each category of commodities, (b) this decision procedure will remain constant over time, as long as his income does not vary significantly in either direction, and (c) the proportions of his total income a consumer allocates to each category will be reflected to a close approximation by the proportions allocated to these categories by those consumers that are in the same social and economic class. This is not to say we are postulating that each consumer must allocate the same proportion of his total annual income to each category of commodities. But rather, that we can postulate the existence of such a decision process. And depending on whether we wish to explain the behavior of a particular group or an individual consumer, we can adjust the relevant parameter values to be consistent with the observed empirical evidence. For example, it is clearly possible to observe the behavior of a particular consumer and note that of his total annual income he allocates 26 per cent to rent or other housing costs, 32 per cent to food, 24 per cent to expenditures on clothing, furniture, and other household items, and the remaining 18 per cent to the expenses of travelling and recreational pursuits. It is also possible to observe in a similar manner the allocative procedures of a particular group of consumers who live in a specified geographical region. Hence, if we wish to be able to explain this allocative process we must construct a decision process in which it is possible to adjust the relevant parameters, so that we may take into account the proportions of more than one individual's allocative procedure.[2]

If we are able to represent the allocation of the consumer's

---

[1] Much of the evidence from recent economic research is reviewed in R. Ferber, *op. cit.* For a particular example of how an allocative procedure is introduced into current utility analysis see: I. F. Pearce, "A Method of Consumer Demand Analysis Illustrated," *Economica*, Vol. **28**, Nov., 1961, pp. 371–394.

[2] It should be noted that the notion of such an allocative decision process is not a novel idea and that Strotz has developed a theoretical formulation of it in current utility analysis; see R. H. Strotz, "The Empirical Implications of a Utility Tree," *Econometrica*, Vol. **25**, 1957, pp. 269–280. See also I. F. Pearce, "An Exact Method of Consumer Demand Analysis," *Econometrica*, Vol. **29**, Oct. 1961.

income between the various categories of commodities we must then examine the decision procedures that govern the spending of the available funds within each category. In this case we shall need to construct decision procedures that govern the expenditure of the funds that have already been allocated to housing, food, clothing, etc. If we require our theory to be able to specify each one of these decision processes it would appear that the theory would have to be somewhat large and complex. However, if there are some similarities between the decision processes required to explain, say, the consumer's decision behavior in the category of food and his decision procedures in some of the other categories, then the task of constructing this theory may not be as formidable as one might previously have expected.

For example, the theory of trust investment is concerned with explaining and predicting the investment behavior of the trust investor while he is selecting a portfolio of common stocks. At the present time the theory does not consider the problem of allocating funds among bonds, preferred stocks and common stocks or the decision procedures that are required if funds are allocated to these categories. Nevertheless, from the evidence presented in this study[3] it would appear that if these decision procedures had been taken into account they would have been constructed out of the decision processes already included in the theory. For a further example of the similarities that appear to exist among the decision processes employed by a human to solve quite different problems consider the principal decision processes that are incorporated in the theory called the General Problem Solver.[4] The General Problem Solver is a theory that represents some of the reasoning processes employed by humans when confronted with the task of solving various types of problems. This theory is principally concerned with the processes of reasoning. And its decision processes contain no references to the subject matter of any particular problem. Hence, if the theory is to be tested by using it to prove some theorems in Euclidean geometry

---

[3] G. P. E. Clarkson, *op. cit.*

[4] For a more detailed description of the structure of the General Problem Solver and of the empirical tests that it has undergone see: A. Newell, J. C. Shaw, and H. A. Simon, "A General Problem Solving Program for a Computer," *op. cit.*, and A. Newell and H. A. Simon, "Simulation of Human Thought," *op. cit.*

the axioms and rules of inference have to be provided before the theory can be employed. That is to say, if the theory is to explain the behavior of a student proving a theorem in Euclidean geometry the initial and boundary conditions would have to include the axioms, rules of inference, and some other basic data about the subject of Euclidean geometry. The same requirements must be met if this theory is to be used to explain the behavior of a subject proving a theorem in mathematical logic, trigonometry, or solving other types of problems that are stated in a particular form.[5]

Thus, it is clear that the decision processes contained in this theory are reasonably independent of the content of the subject matter of the particular problem at hand. From these results there is a certain amount of evidence that suggests that humans use roughly similar sets of decision processes to solve a wide variety of problems.

A. Some Independent Processes

The evidence from this discussion appears to suggest the following points about the consumer's decision processes: (a) the consumer's main decision processes should be roughly the same no matter what category of commodities is being selected from at any one period of time, (b) these decision processes should be constructed so that they are largely independent of the subject matter of any one category of commodities, and (c) some special decision processes will be needed for each category of commodities to allow the basic set of decision process to be applied to the particular decisions that occur only within each of the separate categories. Having arrived at this set of conclusions we shall now move on to examine some of the main decision processes that could be constructed so that they would be largely independent of the subject matter of any one commodity category.

1. The first main decision process that could be constructed in this manner is the consumer's decision to buy a particular set of

---

[5] Since the General Problem Solver reasons in terms of means ends analysis, the problems must be in a form that is suitable to this sort of reasoning process. For a more detailed analysis see the previous references.

commodities with cash or cash equivalents, or by managing to pay for them by a set of monthly payments. This decision process may not appear to be a particularly important one if we take the case of a consumer deciding whether or not to buy some minor durable good. But, if properly constructed there does not seem to be any a priori reason why this decision process could not encompass such decisions as: (a) The decision whether to rent or buy housing accommodation. (In the event that the consumer decides to own his own dwelling unit this process could include the decision on the size of the mortgage payments that could be tolerated. Consequently, it would include a decision on roughly how expensive a dwelling unit the consumer would be willing to purchase.) (b) The decision whether to purchase other durables for cash or whether to spread the payments for them over a period of time. (As in the previous example, this decision process would include some notion of the upper limit of the size of these periodic payments that the consumer would be willing to pay.) And (c) many of the remaining rent or buy decisions that a consumer periodically has to make a decision about, e.g., the "go-now-and-pay-later" plans for vacations, the monthly payment for insurance premiums against various contingencies, etc. This is not to say that all these decisions can be reproduced by one decision process. But rather that they all have one essential element in common—that is, whether there are allocated funds available to cover the purchase of the commodity in question; and if not, whether by paying for the commodity over a period of time the periodic payments will be low enough so that they can be paid for by the funds that have already been allocated to that commodity category. In other words, we are essentially suggesting that there is still another major allocative process which must be taken into account after a consumer has decided on how to allocate his total income among the various categories of commodities. Further, we are suggesting that this second allocative process will be largely independent of the contents of each category. Consequently its main purpose will be to decide by what method of payment the commodities in question are to be purchased, if the total outflow of funds is not to exceed the total amount of funds previously allocated to this commodity category. While this allocative process may differ slightly among particular individuals we are also suggesting that its principal components will be the same, and that the essential parts of this procedure could be represented by one set of decision processes.

For example, if we refer once again to the theory of trust investment, we can see how the analogous situation could be handled in that context. As previously mentioned, the theory of trust investment was only concerned with explaining the decision behavior of a trust investor as it pertained to the selection of common stocks for particular trust accounts. Also we have noted that the consumer's decision to allocate his total income among the various commodity categories is analogous to the trust investor's decision to allocate the total funds available for investment among the various categories of securities. What we are now suggesting is that the decision on how to allocate the funds within each category is essentially the same for all categories. This is not to say that the decision process in the theory of trust investment which governs the selection of common stocks would be identical to the processes which govern the selection of bonds of preferred stocks. But rather that these selection procedures can be represented by one main decision process which allocates the funds among the different common stocks, preferred stocks, and bonds.

In the theory of trust investment there is a set of decision processes which govern the process that identifies the particular set of securities from which a portfolio is selected. But independent of the particular trust account under consideration, there is only one decision procedure which enables the theory to allocate the available funds among the securities that are considered to be appropriate for a specified account. Hence, we are suggesting that if the theory encompassed the selection of bonds and preferred stocks as well, then there still would need to be only one principal decision procedure which determined how the funds available for each category were to be allocated among the available securities. While this hypothesis was not tested, the evidence[6] suggests that such a hypothesis might well be confirmed if it were submitted to a series of empirical tests.

Despite the fact that this evidence does not offer a great deal of support for our hypothesis, it is sufficient to suggest the possible existence of such a decision process. And it must be left to empirical

---

[6] *Op. cit.*, Chapters 6 and 7.

research to determine whether it can be corroborated or not. Also, until some further empirical investigations are carried out, there does not seem to be any reason to suggest that a consumer should behave in a radically different fashion from that of a trust investor. Accordingly, unless some evidence is discovered that refutes our hypothesis, it would appear that the allocation process could be represented by a set of decision processes that was sufficient to account for the allocative procedure within each of the various categories.

2. Another major decision procedure which could be constructed so that it was independent of the content of a particular category is the process that permits the consumer to select one set of commodities from the available alternatives. This is not to say that the set of processes which would allow a consumer to select a collection of groceries should be the same as the set of decision procedures which would allow him to decide which new clothes he should buy. But rather it is the procedure by which these decisions are reached that represents the common element among these many particular decisions. In micro-economic theory this decision procedure is stated in terms of the maximization of a given criterion function. Now a maximizing decision process implies, among other things, that all the available alternatives must be compared against each other. It also implies that after these comparisons are made the consumer then selects the commodity or set of commodities which yield him the highest utility—that is, are the most preferred or in some definable way rank the highest on the comparison scale. Whether a consumer does in fact employ a maximizing decision procedure or not is a question that can only be settled by empirical research. But what we are suggesting is that we can also assume there is one principal set of processes which a consumer employs in order to decide on the particular set of commodities to purchase. That this set of decision processes should turn out to be consistent with a maximizing hypothesis is something, as we have just noted, which can only be determined by empirical research. However, at present the available evidence[7] suggests that this decision procedure would be composed of the following two components:

---

[7] For an empirical exploration of some of the implications of these processes see: J. Feldman, *op. cit.*, and G. P. E. Clarkson, *op. cit.* For further, more general

First of all there would be a set of decision processes that enabled the consumer to rank order, or in some other manner compare, the alternatives that are available within a particular class or sub-class of commodities. This does not imply that the criteria by which each class or sub-class of commodities is compared are to remain the same for all classes and categories of commodities. On the contrary, one would expect a different set of criteria to apply to each sub-class of commodities. For example, one would not expect the criteria employed by a consumer to select his groceries to be the same as those employed when he selects a new refrigerator. The point at issue, though, is not whether a particular set of criteria is employed to rank order a particular sub-class of commodities. But rather it is the process by which these criteria are employed which will remain the same independent of the class or sub-class of commodities that is being considered. For example, in the theory of trust investment a different set of criteria is employed for each of the investment policies to ensure that securities are selected that are consistent with the particular objectives of each trust account, e.g. growth, income, and mixtures of these two goals. But in order to make the desired selections only one basic set of decision processes is employed. Consequently, we are suggesting that the consumer's selection procedure can be represented by one set of decision processes which are constructed so as to allow for the inclusion of particular sets of criteria which in turn depend on the class of commodities currently under consideration.

The second component of this decision procedure would consist of a set of processes that determine the manner in which possible alternatives are to be appraised for selection. If we had a maximizing decision procedure all the available alternatives would have to be searched and examined in order to ensure that the "best" one was selected. However, in our case we are trying to construct the outlines of a theory that would be sufficient to reproduce observed behavior. The evidence that exists[8] suggests that individuals do not exhaustively search and examine all the available alterna-

---

evidence see: R. M. Cyert, H. A. Simon, and D. B. Trow, "Observation of a Business Decision," *Journal of Business*, Vol. **29**, 1956, pp. 237–248; and the cases cited in R. M. Cyert and J. G. March, *The Behavioral Theory of the Firm*.

[8] For examples of this behavior in individuals see the references cited in the

tives. On the contrary, it appears that individuals search among the alternatives until one is found that meets the specified criteria. At this point the search process stops and the satisfactory alternative is selected.

For example, in the theory of trust investment securities are searched and examined until a list of common stocks that are suitable for the investment policy of the trust account under consideration is created. These stocks are classified by industry. Also there is a diversification rule that restricts purchases to no more than one security per industry. As a result, the theory must provide some procedures for selecting the particular participation in each industry. Now a decision rule that required *all* the securities within each industry to be examined before a selection was made would generate behavior patterns that are distinctly different from those produced by a decision rule that started its search at the top of a list and stopped the minute a security was found that met the desired criteria. In the empirical tests, it was the behavior generated by the latter decision rule that more closely matched the observed behavior of the trust investor. Similar evidence is provided in the empirical research noted in the previous footnote. Hence, it would appear that we should adopt for our theory of behavior a decision procedure that allows the consumer to search among the available commodities until one is found that meets the desired criteria for that type of sub-class of commodities.

3. A further major requirement of our theory would be a set of decision processes that allows the theory to adjust its selections in accordance with some expectations about the future behavior of prices, and other variables that are considered important. Once again it is suggested that the basic set of processes that accounts for the consumer's expectations should be independent of the content of a particular commodity category—that is, the chief mechanisms that incorporate and manipulate expectations should be the same no matter what the expectations refer to. In this case the evidence suggests[9] that expectations can be accounted for by

---

previous footnote as well as: A. Newell, J. C. Shaw, and H. A. Simon, "Empirical Explorations . . . ." *op. cit.*

[9] For some examples of this pattern-recognizing process see: Bruner, Goodnow and Austin, *A Study in Thinking*, Wiley, 1956; and J. Feldman, *op. cit.*

decision processes that search for and recognize patterns among the given data. Although the evidence on this point is somewhat sketchy, it appears that one way in which patterns can be built and recognized is to employ the patterns created by past data as the basis from which to interpret the current and the expected movements of a variable.

For example, if the pattern created by the movements of the prices of a particular sub-class of commodities has been constant over the relevant period in the past a sudden rise in these prices would probably be interpreted by this pattern recognizing process as some temporary phenomena which will soon disappear. If, however, the higher price level is maintained for a period of time, and there are no indications that the level will go any lower in the immediate future, then the pattern recognizing process would adjust itself to the new level of prices. Decisions about future price movements would then be made in terms of the new price level. While this is by no means the only type of pattern-recognition process that could be employed, the only way to determine which one should be used is to examine the behavior generated by these processes and see which one comes the closest to matching the observed behavior of consumers. Once a set of decision processes has been constructed that is sufficient to account for the observed behavior, this hypothesis should then be used as the basis for the decision procedures that are to account for the effect of expectations on the consumer's behavior in each category of commodities.

4. A fourth, and perhaps the last, major component that this theory would require is a set of processes that resolved the various conflicting situations that might arise. For example, in any particular time period the amount of funds available for expenditure within a given category of commodities may not be sufficient to cover either the expense of the proposed purchase or the payments that have already been incurred. One method for settling such conflicts before they arise is to include a decision rule that does not allow the total expenditure within each category to exceed the total amount of funds that have previously been allocated for it. If this allocation procedure is carried out each week or month, then when the funds of one category are exhausted the theory would prohibit further purchase until a new allocation was made at the beginning of the next period. While this decision rule may well generate results that are consistent with observed behavior, it is possible that a decision rule which allows available funds to be interchanged between categories might generate behavior patterns that were more consistent with the observed data. In either event a decision rule of this sort is clearly required. And it is up to empirical investigations to discover which one best suits the purposes at hand.

2. INTERPRETING THE PROPOSED THEORY

Having outlined some of the major decision processes that an "ideal" model of a consumer's decision-making behavior would require, we shall now examine the ways in which this "ideal" theory could be employed to establish an explanation of a particular individual's behavior. As we have noted on several occasions, the only way in which a theory representing an "ideal" case can be employed in an explanation of a particular event is by providing a set of interpretive rules that allow the general model to be related to the data of the particular case. In the case of our theory of decision-making behavior these interpretive rules would consist of a collection of statements that prescribed the ways in which the particular tastes, preferences, and other parameter values of the individual are to be incorporated into the decision processes. To clarify how these interpretive rules might be employed we shall examine the main decision mechanisms outlined in the previous section and shall attempt to point out the various factors that should be included if the theory is to be used to account for the behavior of a particular individual.

For the first decision process—that is, the procedure that allocates the consumer's total income among the various categories of commodities—the interpretive rules appear to be readily identifiable. The decision process itself was constructed to allow for the inclusion of particular parameter values. Thus, it would appear that this decision rule could be empirically interpreted by observing the proportions of total income that a consumer allocates to each category and placing these parameter values directly into the decision process. Clearly this would allow our decision rule to account for this consumer's allocative procedure up to that moment when he altered his allocations. While many people may continue to employ one set of allocative procedures with admirable constancy, an inflexible decision rule would prevent the theory from responding to changes in total income with disproportionate changes in the allocations. Hence it would appear that some set of adaptive mechanisms should be included that allows the proportions of the total income spent on various commodity categories to change as the total income rises or falls. One possibility is to include in this decision procedure a set of pattern recognition processes. If this type of process was employed a sudden rise in income could be treated as though it were an unearned bonus to be allocated to some special purchase.[10] On the other hand a steady rise in income would be treated as the normal pattern to be expected and the allocative procedure would carry on in the same manner as before. Whichever set of decision processes is selected the parameter values can be determined from a detailed study of consumer behavior. Therefore, for this decision process the interpretive rules would consist of a set of statements that described how the observed allocative behavior of a particular consumer was to be reflected by a particular set of parameter values.

Although the principal allocative process that we have just discussed does not seem to present too many obstacles to empirical interpretation, the second allocative procedure—namely, the decision procedure that decides whether to pay for purchases out of immediate income or by several payments over a period of time— would require more extensive empirical investigation. It has been suggested that the allocative procedure in each category of commodities could be represented by one basic decision process. While this may in fact turn out to be the case the decision of whether to "pay now or over a period of time" will in part depend on various

[10] Such behavior would not be inconsistent with the "permanent income hypothesis" of M. Friedman, *A Theory of the Consumption Function*, National Bureau of Economic Research, Princeton, 1957, or the "permanent wealth', hypothesis of F. Modigliani and A. Ando, "The 'Permanent Income' and the 'Life Cycle' Hypotheses of Saving Behavior," in I. Friend and R. Jones (ed.) *Proceedings of the Conference on Consumption and Saving*, University of Pennsylvania, Vol. II, 1960, pp. 49–174.

factors, e.g., the interest rate, the amount of credit already out-standing, the full cost of the commodity, etc., which can be expected to vary from one period to the next. Hence, not only must the decision process itself make allowances for the inclusion of these variables, but the interpretive rules must specify a set of procedures whereby the appropriate parameter values may be empirically determined. Unfortunately this part of the decision-making process has not been sufficiently explored to suggest in any detail the types of interpretive rules that might be required. But one possibility is a decision rule that discovers whether a further set of time payments can be allowed by evaluating whether the total amount of outstanding credit exceeds a certain proportion of total income. While this particular decision rule may or may not be corroborated by empirical research the interpretation of such a rule would not present any serious obstacles.

In a similar manner interpretive rules would have to be supplied for the remaining decision processes. For example, the relevant attributes of various classes and sub-classes of commodities would have to be observed and noted so that the theory's selection procedures could compare the available commodities on the same basis as that of the particular consumer under investigation. Also some criteria would have to be incorporated into the theory to enable it to recognize when a particular commodity was considered to be satisfactory. Presumably some of these criteria would vary with the different classes of commodities and we might be led to expect a rather complex set of criteria for each class and category. But, if the selection procedures of the theory of trust investment are at all representative of human decision-making processes, these selection procedures should neither be highly complex nor differ too much from one class of commodities to another. The same comments should also apply to the sets of decision processes that account for the effects of expectations on purchasing decisions. While each category of commodities may require its own set of pattern recognition processes it is somewhat unlikely that they will differ in any radical way. Some variables may be more important for one class of commodities than another. But the total number of important variables for any class of commodities will not be large. Thus, they should not be particularly difficult either to identify or interpret.

While the answers to these problems, and hence the specification of these interpretive rules, can only be obtained by empirical research, it would be somewhat premature to conclude that the task was too involved or complex to be successfully undertaken. In discussing the construction of this theory we have repeatedly noted the research on human decision-making behavior that is already underway. Also we have freely employed the evidence from some of these studies to suggest various ways in which the proposed theory can be simplified and empirically interpreted. Further, since several of the reported theories have survived a series of direct empirical tests, there is a certain amount of evidence to suggest that a detailed theory of a consumer's decision behavior can in fact be constructed and tested. Therefore, although a considerable amount of research still needs to be undertaken there does not appear to be any *prima facie* reason why part of this research should not result in a testable theory of consumer behavior.

3. ON REDUCING THE THEORY OF DEMAND

In the previous section we have outlined in some detail the possible structure and content of a testable theory of consumer decision-making behavior. It is now time to examine more closely the problems involved in determining how the theories of utility and demand could be reduced to such a theory of individual decision-making behavior.

The proof that one theory can be reduced to another is a problem that can only be settled by empirical research. It is only after a theory has been constructed that it can be effectively demonstrated that the laws and postulates of one theory can in fact be deduced from another. But, we have suggested that one way of turning the theories of utility and demand into empirically testable theories is to develop a testable theory of consumer decision behavior to which these theories can be reduced. Therefore, it is still part of our task to point out the manner in which this reduction process might be shown to have taken place. Although we cannot demonstrate that this reduction has been accomplished, we are at least able to examine some of the ways in which such a reduction could take place.

If we are to be able to demonstrate that a micro-reduction of the theory of demand has been effected, then we clearly must be able to show that the reduction of the theory of utility has also been accomplished. But, if we can show how the theory of utility could be reduced, then it would follow that the theory of demand would have been similarly reduced. To be able to micro-reduce the theory of utility implies that the postulates of utility theory must be derivable from the reducing theory. Accordingly, if we can demonstrate that it would be possible to derive the postulates of utility theory from our theory of consumer decision-making behavior, then it would follow that the theories of utility and demand had been effectively reduced. Our task, then, is to examine the theory of consumer behavior as outlined in the previous sections in order to ascertain whether it would be possible to deduce from this theory the basic postulates of utility theory. However, before we can proceed with this investigation we must first be sure that we understand not only what the theory of utility represents but also how its postulates may be interpreted.

As noted in Chapter 3, the theory of utility is a theory of decision-making behavior and can be taken to represent how the "ideal" consumer selects the bundle of commodities that he desires from all of the alternatives that confront him. But, in Chapters 4 and 5 it was pointed out that this theory lacked sufficient empirical interpretation to be subjected to a series of empirical tests. One of the difficulties that was encountered was the fact that it is not possible, except in a few simplified cases,[11] to specify beforehand the decision-making behavior that the consumer must exhibit if it is to be consistent with the basic postulates. But now that we have, at least in outline form, a theory that proposes to account for a consumer's choice behavior in terms of his decision-making processes. It would appear that we have a theory that will specify in some detail the decision behavior that the consumer must exhibit if he is to behave in a manner that is consistent with our theory. Thus, if we can accept for the moment the hypothesis that we can indeed construct and test our theory, then we can examine the behavior that is generated by the theory to see whether it is in fact consistent with the basic postulates of utility theory. This is not to say that the postulates of utility theory would necessarily be

---

[11] For example, the binary choice experiment, see pp. 77–79.

directly testable in this manner. But this approach does suggest a possible way in which they might be tested.

Consider, for example, the first three postulates as noted in Chapter 3. The first requires that the consumer must be able to state for all possible pairs of alternatives A and B whether he prefers A to B, B to A, or whether he is indifferent between them. Now our theory of consumer behavior does not necessarily examine all possible alternatives before it applies its selection procedures. Instead it only examines some of those alternatives that are available to it at the time the decision is to be made. However, the theory of revealed preference has shown that it is not crucial to the theory of utility that *all* possible alternatives be examined. Thus, if we examine only those alternatives that are considered by our theory at one period of time, we can still check to see whether the preferences exhibited by the theory are consistent with a weak ordering of the alternatives. Now the second and third postulates require the consumer to be consistent in his choices and to make up his mind whether for a particular pair of alternatives A and B he prefers A to B, B to A, or is indifferent between them. Once again the decision behavior generated by our theory could be examined to ascertain whether it was consistent with these postulates or not.

For example, the processes that order and make selections from a certain class of commodities can be inspected to see whether the selections that they generate corroborate these two postulates of utility theory. Any changes in these selections that are due to a change in expectations could also be inspected for consistency. Hence, although we cannot demonstrate that these postulates could be derived directly from our proposed theory it does appear that it would be possible to subject them to a series of indirect empirical tests.

The testing of the fourth postulate—that is, whether the consumer always selects that set of commodities that he most prefers— would, however, appear to present some rather special difficulties. Earlier in this chapter it was noted that a maximizing decision criterion implies that the selection procedures must examine all the available alternatives, so that it can ensure that the "best" one has been selected. In our proposed theory of consumer behavior the selection procedure stops as soon as an alternative is discovered that meets the appropriate criteria. Under this decision rule it is quite possible to accept the very first alternative that is examined. If the behavior generated by this decision function is consistent with the observed behavior of consumers, then this evidence would not appear to be consistent with that required by the fourth postulate.[12] However, to be able to corroborate or disconfirm the maximizing postulate one would have to be able to show that the alternative selected by our theory was or was not the "best" one that could have been selected from those available at the time. This would imply that the selection process contained criteria that were sufficient to identify the "best" commodity from those that were available. But the proposed selection procedures only reflect the adequacy of the alternatives to meet a set of criteria that are adjusted to meet changing expectations. And there does not seem to be any direct way of deciding whether the selected alternatives are "optimal" or not. Manifestly, this is a question that can only, at best, be settled by empirical research. If it should turn out that a maximizing decision criterion is not consistent with the observed behavior then either the fourth postulate must be relaxed,[13] or our proposed micro-reduction of the theories of utility and demand cannot take place. If the latter alternative is chosen we are back to where we began and are faced with an untestable theory of demand. If the former alternative is accepted and the consequences explored then the evidence strongly suggests that a testable, revised theory of demand can indeed be developed.[14]

---

[12] For a more detailed comparison of the behavior generated by a decision function of this type and a maximizing decision criterion see: G. P. E. Clarkson, *op. cit.*, Chapter 8; and J. Feldman, *op. cit.*

[13] For an example of a rational theory of choice that does not employ a maximizing decision criterion see: H. A. Simon, "A Behavioral Model of Rational Choice," *Quarterly Journal of Economics*, Vol. **69**, Feb., 1955 (reprinted in H. A. Simon, *Models of Man*, 1957, pp. 241–260).

[14] See, for example, the evidence that is presented to support the development of a more comprehensive and testable theory of the firm that is contained in: R. M. Cyert and J. G. March, *The Behavioral Theory of the Firm.*

Summary and Conclusions

At the beginning of this essay we observed that the theories of economics are noted for their lack of success in predicting the course of economic events. Also it was pointed out that it has frequently been argued that the problems involved in the development and testing of economic theory are essentially different from those encountered in the physical sciences. It has been the purpose of this study to dispute and refute this point of view. In particular it has been our primary aim to demonstrate that it is within the theories of economics themselves, and not within the content of the subject matter itself, that the source of the difficulty lies.

To demonstrate the validity of this claim we pointed out that if it could be shown that the theories of economics could not be subjected to a process of refutation by empirical test, then it would follow that these theories have been constructed in a manner that precludes the possibility of generating successful predictions. While we have by no means demonstrated the validity of this claim for all economic theories we elected to present the evidence for our claim in terms of one of its acknowledged goals—namely, the description and prediction of the behavior of economic man. Consequently, in the first part of this essay it has been our object to investigate and establish the proposition that the micro-economic theory of consumer behavior (the theory of demand) is not refutable by empirical test.

Although it is usually more difficult to substantiate a negative rather than a positive claim we saw from the analysis of deductive systems that a theory could not be refuted by empirical test if it is constructed in such a fashion that: (a) all its hypotheses and concepts are stated in terms of theoretical concepts, or, (b) not one of its basic postulates or deduced hypotheses can be directly refuted by empirical test. Hence, our first task was to examine the terms and concepts employed in the theory of demand in order to ascertain the extent of their empirical content. This analysis was carried out by examining both the way in which the concepts are introduced into the theory and the way in which they are related to one another. By this analysis it was evinced that the concepts and terms of the theory of demand depended for their empirical content on the four basic postulates of utility theory. This is not to say that there are no other means of introducing empirical content into these concepts. But rather that the remaining sources of empirical content could be employed only if these basic postulates were empirically confirmed. It was concluded, therefore, that the concepts of the theory of demand were open to empirical analysis if and only if the basic postulates themselves could be confirmed by empirical test.

Once the concepts had been examined by themselves it was then necessary to inspect both the basic postulates and the deduced hypotheses. The object was to determine whether either one or both of these sets of hypothesized expressions could be corroborated by empirical test. If either set of statements could pass this test then it would follow that the concepts of the theory would have some empirical content. And, as a result the theory itself could be confirmed or disconfirmed by empirical test. But, an examination of the function of general laws or hypotheses in the scientific explanation of observable events led us to the conclusion that neither the basic postulates nor the hypothesized expressions had sufficient empirical interpretation to permit them to be disconfirmed by empirical test. Despite the fact that empirical evidence can be found that tends to support these hypotheses it was demonstrated that it would not be possible to employ any of these observations to disconfirm these hypotheses.

In our discussion of deductive systems it was noted that a "true" consequent can be used to support a "false" premiss just as readily as a "true" one. Thus, unless it is possible, in principle, to disconfirm these hypotheses we have no means of determining whether they have been confirmed or not.

Since the hypothesized statements cannot be disconfirmed it follows that the explanations of consumer behavior offered by the theory of demand must fit an *ex post facto* explanatory schema. In other words, the theoretical structure of the theory of demand is such that it is an effective tool for analyzing and rationalizing the occurrence of an event *after, but not before*, it has occurred. Further, if the theory of demand is unable to establish a scientific explanation of observed consumer behavior, then it is not possible to employ this theory to generate scientifically meaningful predictions. By demonstrating that the theory of demand is an uninterpreted theoretical structure we established the first part of our thesis— namely, that the reason for the absence of predictability in micro-economics lies within the theory of demand itself, and not within some special properties of the subject matter.

Once it has been shown that the theory of demand cannot be refuted by empirical test the question is immediately raised of how to rescue the theory from beyond the pale of empirical science. From our analysis it appears that this problem would be resolved if a set of postulates were constructed that was both directly refutable by empirical test and formulated in such a manner that it formed an empirical basis for the theory of demand. Although it is quite unlikely that there is only one solution to this dilemma the theory of reduction suggests one possible answer. In brief, this theory suggests that an answer can be found by developing a testable theory of individual consumer behavior to which the theory of demand can be micro-reduced. In other words, the empirical basis of the theory of demand can possibly be found in a testable theory of individual decision-making behavior.

In the last part of this essay a solution to the dilemma is proposed by developing the outlines of a theory of individual consumer behavior. This theory is designed to serve as a basis for the micro-reduction of the theory of demand to observable decision-making behavior. While the actual construction and testing of such a micro-reduction theory can only be accomplished by empirical research, recent developments in the theory of human problem solving were examined to discover whether theories of decision-making could be corroborated by empirical test. Despite the fact that several of these theories are concerned only with human problem solving and not with economics at all, it was evinced that hypotheses concerning decision-making behavior could be confirmed in a wide variety of empirical contexts. If it is possible to construct a testable theory of human problem solving, then it follows that it is possible to construct a testable theory of individual consumer behavior. Clearly, the successful reduction of the theory of demand to a testable theory of individual decision-making behavior can only be accomplished by empirical research. But it has been our object to point out that a micro-reduction of the theory of demand is both theoretically and empirically justified.

Once the theory of demand is successfully reduced it is clear that the more common objections to developing testable economic theories will have been shown to be false. For example, economists, along with many other social scientists, have often stated that the inability to conduct controlled experiments is one of the major obstacles preventing the discovery and development of testable theories. But, if an empirical basis for existing theoretical structures is sought by developing theories of individual behavior the problem of running controlled experiments almost entirely disappears. From the evidence adduced in support of our theory of individual consumer behavior it is apparent that human decision-making can be described and incorporated into a testable theory of economic behavior. (It bears repeating that these theories have been developed by employing the theory of human problem solving and the technique of computer simulation. And the technique of simulation allows these theories to be repeatedly tested and amended to fit a wide variety of observed behavior.) Now a particular theory may only be concerned with the behavior of an individual consumer under a particular set of circumstances. But if the theory is empirically testable, then it can be tested against repeated observations of the same consumers. While we have no desire to minimize the difficulties that will be encountered in such a testing program, the point at issue is that the theory can be subjected to such a testing process. Therefore, even though controlled experiments on a grand scale will probably always present enormous difficulties, the mere existence of a theory that can be subjected to a rigorous series of empirical tests refutes the hypothesis that it is not possible to test an economic theory by such experimental procedures.

The possibility of reducing the theory of demand to a testable theory of individual consumer behavior raises a further and more important question—namely, that of the direction of future research in micro-economics. Since the theory of demand and the theory of utility serve as the basis for a large part of micro-economic theory, the results of our analysis imply that a large part of micro-economics is also not refutable by empirical test. While this is not the first time that this conclusion has been voiced the existence of a possible solution to the dilemma suggests that more attention should be paid to the implications generated by this state of affairs.

Traditionally economists have been more interested in developing normative rather than positive theories. But it is clear that it is the positive theories that must provide the scientific basis for policy prescriptions. If the theories of micro-economics cannot be subjected to empirical test then it follows that their normative counter-parts must also be largely devoid of empirical content. Indeed, before it is possible to employ normative theories to generate empirically meaningful policies, the positive theories upon which these normative theories are based must be empirically confirmed. Therefore, if the chief goal of the economist is to be served, then a great deal more attention must be paid to developing and testing the positive theories of micro-economics.

In this essay, our principal objective has been to isolate and identify the reasons for the lack of predictive success that is so frequently a part of economic theories. We have been led by our analysis to propose a solution to this dilemma. Although our solution has yet to be corroborated by empirical research it is clear from our analysis that the problems of developing and testing micro-economic theory need no longer be considered to be different from those encountered in the physical sciences. Also, and perhaps what is more important, we are able to conclude that it is possible to develop a body of micro-economic theory that has the same predictive and explanatory power as is enjoyed by the physical sciences.

Bibliography

Braithwaite, R. B., *Scientific Explanation*. Cambridge University Press, 1953.

Bridgman, P. W., *The Logic of Modern Physics*. New York: Macmillan, 1927.

Bruner, J. S., J. J. Goodnow, and G. A. Austin, *A Study of Thinking*. New York: John Wiley & Sons, 1956.

Carnap, R., "Testability and Meaning," *Philosophy of Science*, 3: 4 (1936).

———, "Foundations of Logic and Mathematics," *International Encyclopedia of Unified Science*. University of Chicago Press, I: 3 (1939).

———, "On Inductive Logic," *Philosophy of Science*, 12 (1945).

———, "Remarks on Induction and Truth," *Philosophy and Phenomenological Research*, 6 (1946), 590–602.

———, "Statistical and Inductive Probability," in E. H. Madden, ed., *The Structure of Scientific Thought*. Boston: Houghton, 1960.

Church, A., *Introduction to Mathematical Logic*. Princeton: Princeton University Press, 1956.

Clarkson, G. P. E., *Portfolio Selection: A Simulation of Trust Investment*. Englewood Cliffs, N. J.: Prentice-Hall, 1962.

Cyert, R. M. and J. G. March, "Organizational Structure and Pricing Behavior in an Oligopolistic Market," *American Economic Review*, 45 (1955), 129–39.

———, Simon, H. A., and D. B. Trow, "Observations of a Business Decision," *Journal of Business*, 29 (1956), 237–48.

———, Feigenbaum, E. A., and J. G. March, "Models in a Behavioral Theory of the Firm," *Behavioral Science*, 4 (April 1959), 81–95.

———, and J. G. March, *The Behavioral Theory of the Firm*. Englewood Cliffs, N. J.: Prentice-Hall, 1963.

Feigenbaum, E. A., "The Simulation of Verbal Learning Behavior," *Proceedings of the Western Joint Computer Conference*, 19 (May 1961), 121–32. Reprinted in E. A. Feigenbaum and J. Feldman, eds., *Computers and Thought*. New York: McGraw-Hill, 1963.

Feigl, H., "Operationism and Scientific Method," *Psychological Review*, 52 (Sept. 1945), 250–59.

Feldman, J., "Simulation of Behavior in the Binary Choice Experiment," *Proceedings of the Western Joint Computer Conference*, 19 (May 1961), 133–144. Reprinted in E. A. Feigenbaum and J. Feldman, eds., *Computers and Thought*. New York: McGraw-Hill, 1963.

Ferber, R., "Research on Household Behavior," *American Economic Review*, 52 (March 1962), 19–63.

Freidman, M. and L. J. Savage, "The Utility Analysis of Choices Involving Risk," *Journal of Political Science*, **56** (August 1948). Reprinted in the American Economic Review, *Readings in Price Theory*, Homewood, Ill.: Irwin, 1952.

———, *Essays in Positive Economics*. Chicago: University of Chicago Press, 1953.

———, *A Theory of the Consumption Function*. Princeton: National Bureau of Economic Research, Princeton University Press, 1957.

Gelernter, H. L., J. R. Hansen, and D. W. Loveland, "Empirical Explorations of the Geometry Theorem Machine," *Proceedings of the Western Joint Computer Conference* (1960), pp. 143–59.

Grunberg, E., "Notes on the Verifiability of Economic Laws," *Philosophy of Science*, **24** (1957), 337–48.

Hempel, C. G., "The Function of General Laws in History," *Journal of Philosophy*, **39** (1942), pp. 35–48. Reprinted in H. Feigl and W. Sellars, *Readings in Philosophical Analysis*. New York: Appleton, 1949.

——— and P. Oppenheim, "A Definition of 'Degree of Confirmation,' " *Philosophy of Science*, **12**: 2 (1945), 98–115.

———, "Problems and Changes in the Empirical Criterion of Meaning," *Revue Internationale de Philosophie*, Vol. 11, 1950. Reprinted in L. Linsky, ed., *Semantics and the Philosophy of Language*. Urbana: University of Illinois Press, 1952.

———, "The Fundamentals of Concept Formation in Empirical Science," *International Encyclopedia of Unified Science*. Chicago: University of Chicago Press, **II**: 7 (1952).

———, "The Theoretician's Dilemma," *Minnesota Studies in the Philosophy of Science*, Vol. II. Minneapolis: University of Minnesota Press, 1958, pp. 37–98.

———, "The Logic of Functional Analysis," in L. Gross, ed., *Symposium on Sociological Theory*. New York: Row, Peterson, 1959, pp. 271–307.

———, "Deductive-Nomological vs. Statistical Explanation," in H. Feigl *et al.*, eds., *Minnesota Studies in the Philosophy of Science*, Vol. III. Minneapolis: University of Minnesota Press, 1962.

Henderson, J. M. and R. E. Quandt, *Microeconomic Theory*. New York: McGraw-Hill, 1958.

Hicks, J. R., *A Revision of Demand Theory*. New York: Oxford University Press, 1956.

Hutchison, T. W., *The Significance and Basic Postulates of Economic Theory*. London: Macmillan, 1938.

———, "Professor Machlup on Verification in Economics," *Southern Economic Journal*, **XXII** (1955), 476–84.

Kemeny, J. G. and P. Oppenheim, "Systematic Power," *Philosophy of Science*, **22** (1955), 27–33.

Machlup, F., "The Problem of Verification in Economics," *Southern Economic Journal*, **XXII** (July 1955), 1–21.

———, "Rejoinder to a Reluctant Ultra-Empiricist," *Southern Economic Journal*, **XXII** (1955), 485–93.

Mill, J. S., *Essays on Some Unsettled Questions of Political Economy*. London School of Economics and Political Science, Reprint No. 7, 1948.

Von Mises, L., *Human Action: A Treatise on Economics*. New Haven: Yale University Press, 1949.

Midigliani, F. and A. Ando, "The 'Permanent Income' and the 'Life Cycle' Hypotheses of Saving and Behavior," in I. Friend and R. Jones, eds., *Proceedings of the Conference on Consumption and Saving*. Philadelphia: University of Pennsylvania Press, **II** (1960), 49–174.

Nagel, E., "The Meaning of Reduction in the Natural Sciences," in R. C. Stauffer, ed., *Science and Civilization*. Madison: University of Wisconsin Press, 1949.

Newell, A., J. C. Shaw, and H. A. Simon, "Empirical Exploration of the Logic Theory Machine," *Proceedings of the Western Joint Computer Conference* (Feb. 1957), pp. 218–30.

———, "Chess-Playing Program and the Problem of Complexity," *IBM Journal of Research and Development*, Oct. 1958, pp. 320–35.

———, "Elements of a Theory of Human Problem Solving," *Psychological Review*, **65** (1958), 151–66.

———, "A General Problem Solving Program for a Computer," *Computers and Automation*, **8** (July 1960), 10–17.

Newell, A. and H. A. Simon, "The Simulation of Human Thought," *Current Trends in Psychological Theory*. Pittsburgh: University of Pittsburgh Press, 1961, pp. 152–79.

Oppenheim, P. and H. Putnam, "Unity of Science," in H. Feigl *et al.*, eds., *Minnesota Studies in the Philosophy of Science*, Vol. II. Minneapolis: University of Minnesota Press, 1958.

Orcutt, G. H., M. Shubik, G. P. E. Clarkson, and H. A. Simon, "Simulation: a Symposium," *American Economic Review*, **50** (Dec. 1960), 894–932.

Papandreou, A. G., *Economics as a Science*. Lippincott, 1958.

Pearce, I. F., "An Exact Method of Consumer Demand Analysis," *Econometrica*, **29** (1961).

———, "A Method of Consumer Demand Analysis Illustrated," *Economica*, **28** (1961), 371–394.

Popper, K. R., *The Logic of Scientific Discovery*. New York: Basic Books, 1959.

Reichenbach, H., *Philosophical Foundation of Quantum Mechanics.* Berkeley: University of California Press, 1944.

Robbins, L., *An Essay on the Nature and Significance of Economic Science.* 2nd ed. London: Macmillan, 1935.

Samuelson, P. A., *Foundations of Economic Analysis.* Cambridge: Harvard University Press, 1947.

Schoeffler, S., *The Failure of Economics: A Diagnostic Study.* Cambridge: Harvard University Press, 1955.

Schultz, H., *The Theory and Measurement of Demand.* Chicago: University of Chicago Press, 1938.

Simon, H. A., "A Behavioral Model of Rational Choice," *Quarterly Journal of Economics,* **69** (Feb. 1955). Reprinted in H. A. Simon, *Models of Man.* New York: John Wiley & Sons, 1957, pp. 241–260.

Slutsky, E. E., "On the Theory of the Budget of the Consumer," American Economic Review, *Readings in Price Theory.* Homewood, Ill.: Irwin, 1952, pp. 27–56.

Strotz, R. H., "The Empirical Implications of a Utility Tree," *Econometrica,* **25** (1957), 269–280.

Index

A

Analytic definition, 50
Ando, A., 134n
Austin, G. A., 131n

B

Binary choice experiment, 77–78, 137n
Braithwaite, R. B., 18–19, 52n
Bridgman, P. W., 22n
Bruner, J. S., 131n
Budget equation, 33

C

Calculus, as a deductive system, 12–19
  completeness, 14
  consistency, 14
  interpretation, 17–18
  meta-language, 15
  object language, 15
  primitive symbols, 13, 15
  proof, 14, 16
  rules of inference, 13, 16
  semantics, 12
  syntax, 12
  truth tables, 17–18
  well-formed formulas, 13, 15–16
Carnap, R., 12n, 66n, 95n
Church, A., 16n
Clarkson, G. P. E., 109n, 110n, 125n,
    129n, 139n
Complement, 42
  interpretation, 59
Concepts, definition of, 47–53
  analytic, 50
  nominal, 48
  real, 49–50
  theoretical, 52
Concepts, interpretation of, 50–53
  empirical analysis, 51
  meaning analysis, 50
Confirmation, degree of, 71
Contingent propositions, 19–20
Cyert, R. M., 109n, 130n, 139n

D

Decision processes, 122–136
  allocation of funds, 126–128, 133–135
  conflict resolution, 132–133
  pattern recognition (expectations),
    131–132
  selection procedures, 129–131, 135
Deductive systems, 12–19
  applied, 19
  interpreted, 17–19
  pure, 18
  uninterpreted, 13–14
Demand curves, 37–42, 59–62, 79–83
  definition of, 37–38, 60
  empirical analysis of, 80–83
  interpretation of, 60–62
Disconfirmation, criteria for, 71–72

E

Economist's dilemma, 101, 103
Empirical analysis, 51
Empirical hypothesis, 70
Empirical law, 68
Explanation:
  by decision processes, 113–114, 117
  economic, 84–85
  historic events, 97–98
  ill-specified events, 69
  meta-economic, 99–100
  probabilistic, 93–96
  scientific, 67
  well-specified event, 69

F

Falsifiability criterion, 21–22
Feigenbaum, E. A., 109n, 116n
Feigl, H., 22n, 93n
Feldman, J., 116n, 129n, 139n
Ferber, R., 81n, 124n
Friedman, M., 88n, 91n, 134n
Friend, I., 134n

G

Gelernter, H. L., 115n
General law, 65–66
General hypothesis, 70
General Problem Solver, 125
Goodnow, J. J., 131n
Gross, L., 11n
Grunberg, E., 83n, 109n

H

Hansen, J. R., 115n
Hempel, C. G., 11n, 22n, 23n, 47n, 65n,
    71n, 93n
Henderson, J. M., 27n
Hicks, J. R., 30n, 44n, 74n
Hutchison, T. W., 3n, 6n
Hypothesis:
  as a decision process, 115–116
  empirical, 70
  general, 70
  probabilistic, 94

I

Income effect, 39–40, 61–62
  empirical analysis of, 81–82
Indifference curve, 31–32
  interpretation, 55–56
  slope, 32
Inferior good, 41

J

Jevons, W. S., 28
Jones, R., 134n

K

Kemeny, J. G., 105n

L

Law:
  empirical, 68
  general, 65–66
  ideal, 74
    interpretation of, 74–79
Linsky, L., 23n

Logic of prediction, 89–92
Loveland, D. W., 115n

M

Machlup, F., 3n, 100n
Madden, E. H., 95n
March, J. G., 109n, 130n, 139n
Marginalist controversy, 88n, 100n
Marshall, A., 28
Maxwell, G., 22n, 93n
Meaning analys s, 50
Meta-economics, 99–100
Meta-language, 15
Micro-reduction, 105–109
  postulates of utility theory, 138–139
  theories of utility and demand, 109–118
Mill, J. S., 88n
Mises, Von L., 100n
Modigliani, F., 135n
Morgenstern, O., 73n, 75, 78

N

Nagel, E., 104n
Neumann, Von, 73n, 75, 78
Newell, A., 109n, 110, 115n, 116n, 125n,
    131n
Nominal definition, 48

O

Object language, 15
Operationism, 22
Oppenheim, P., 71n, 105n
Orcutt, G. H., 109n

P

Papandreou, A. G., 6n, 85n
Pearce, I., 124n
Popper, K. R., 21n, 66n
Postulates of Utility Theory, 29
  empirical analysis, 73–79
  statement in conditional form, 73
Postulates of Theory of Human Problem
    Solving, 110
  interpretation, 110–111
Prediction:
  by decision processes, 113–114, 117

Prediction (*cont.*)
  economic, 91–92
  logic of, 89–90
  probabilistic, 93–96
  scientific, 70–71
Propositional calculus, 15
Putnam, H., 105n

Q

Quandt, R. E., 27n

R

Real definition, 49–50
Reduction, 104–109
  one branch of science to another, 105
  one theory to another, 105, 107–108
  postulates of utility theory, 138–139
  theory of, 105
Reichenbach, H., 71n
Robbins, L., 100n

S

Samuelson, P. A., 42n, 46n
Savage, L. J., 91n
Schoeffler, S., 4n
Schrödinger, 52n, 70
Schultz, H., 81n
Scientific explanation, 67
Scientific prediction, 70–71
Scriven, M., 22n
Shaw, J. C., 109n, 110, 115n, 116n, 125n, 131n
Shubik, M., 109n
Simon, H. A., 109n, 110, 115n, 116n, 125n, 130n, 131n, 139n
Slutsky, E. E., 39n
Slutsky equation, 39
Stauffer, R. C., 104n
Strotz, R. H., 124n
Substitute, 42
  interpretation, 59
Substitution effect, 39–40
  empirical analysis, 81–82

T

Tautology, truth value, 18
Testability, hypotheses and laws, 70
Theoretical concepts, 52
Theory of human problem solving, 110–112
  empirical analysis, 112–117
  empirical tests for, 114–115, 117–118
  postulates defined, 110
  postulates interpreted, 110–111
Theory of individual consumer behavior, 122–139
  as an ideal theory, 123, 133
  as a reduction theory, 121–122, 136–139
  decision processes, 122–136
    allocation of funds, 126–128, 133–135
    conflict resolution, 132–133
    expectations, 131–132
    selection procedures, 129–131, 135
Theory of reduction, 104–108
Theory of revealed preference, 42–45
  postulates for, 43–44
Trow, D. B., 130n
Truth tables, 17–18

U

Utility:
  cardinal, 28
  ordinal, 28–29
  principle of diminishing marginal, 28
Utility function:
  analytic definition, 54–55
  classical definition, 29–30
  monotonicity, 37
  postulates for, 29, 55
  real definition, 54
Utility maximization:
  definition, 33–36, 57
  first order condition, 34
  postulates for, 34–36, 58
  second order condition, 35–36
Utility theory, 28–37
  postulates for, 29
    conditional form, 73
    empirical analysis, 73–79

W

Walras, L., 28